Speeches from the Desk of the Principal
(Driving Growth and Success in the Life of a Student)

OrangeBooks Publication

1st Floor, Rajhans Arcade, Mall Road, Kohka, Bhilai, Chhattisgarh 490020

Website: **www.orangebooks.in**

© Copyright, 2024, Author

All rights reserved. No part of this book may be reproduced, stored in a retrieval system, or transmitted, in any form by any means, electronic, mechanical, magnetic, optical, chemical, manual, photocopying, recording or otherwise, without the prior written consent of its writer.

First Edition, 2024

SPEECHES
FROM THE DESK OF THE
PRINCIPAL

Driving Growth and Success
in the Life of a Student

PRASHANT KUMAR LAL

OrangeBooks Publication
www.orangebooks.in

About The Book

"Speeches from the Desk of the Principal"

(Driving Growth and Success in the Life of a Student)

Welcome to a collection of empowering speeches designed to shape the journey of our students towards becoming knowledgeable, culturally aware, and wholesome individuals. As a principal of an esteemed institutions, it is their privilege to guide and inspire the students through these assembly speeches, fostering values of discipline, knowledge, and cultural appreciation.

Purpose of the Book

This book serves as a beacon of wisdom and guidance, offering 100 speeches covering a spectrum of topics including festivals, national and international days of importance. Each speech is meticulously crafted to instill a sense of pride in one's culture while nurturing a desire for continuous growth and success.

Goals and Objectives

Cultural Respect and Understanding: Through these speeches, we aim to cultivate a deep appreciation for diverse cultures, fostering an environment of inclusivity and respect.

Personal Growth and Development: By imparting knowledge and wisdom, we empower students to develop into well-rounded individuals capable of facing life's challenges with confidence and resilience.

Preparation for Success: Beyond the realm of academia, this book equips students with essential skills for various competitive exams, public speaking engagements, debates, declarations, and essay writing competitions.

Key Features

Comprehensive Knowledge: Each speech is rich in content, providing students with a holistic understanding of the significance behind festivals, national celebrations, and global events.

Practical Applications: Beyond theoretical knowledge, students will learn practical skills such as effective communication, critical thinking, and persuasive writing, essential for success in today's world.

Inspiration and Motivation: Through anecdotes, examples, and motivational messages, these speeches serve as a source of inspiration, igniting the spark of ambition within each student.

Conclusion

As we embark on this journey together, let us embrace the transformative power of education and strive to create a community of lifelong learners who not only excel academically but also contribute meaningfully to society. With these speeches as our guide, let us pave the way for a future filled with growth, success, and boundless possibilities.

Preface

In the dynamic sphere of education, the role of a principal extends far beyond the administrative corridors. This compilation of, "Speeches from the Desk of the Principal," is a testament to the pivotal responsibility bestowed upon educational leaders in shaping the ethos of an institution. As the orchestrators of a school's intellectual symphony, principals play a crucial role in not only fostering an environment of academic excellence but also in cultivating a robust value system.

This collection encapsulates a diverse array of speeches, ranging from commemorations of religious, national, to international significance. The objective is clear - to enlighten and engage students, teachers, and the entire school community in meaningful dialogues that transcend the confines of the classroom. A principal's duty goes beyond the administrative logistics; it involves the profound task of nurturing minds and hearts.

Within these pages, you will find insights into the comprehensive approach a principal takes to not only train the dedicated staff but also to empower students with knowledge that extends beyond textbooks. Each speech serves as a beacon, guiding the educational journey towards a culture of collaboration, understanding, and respect. It is in these moments of shared reflection that the seeds of a thriving work environment are sown.

As we delve into these speeches, let us recognize the pivotal role a principal that plays in sculpting a holistic educational experience. May these words echo with the collective spirit of our school community, fostering an environment where enlightenment and values interlace to shape the future leaders of tomorrow.

Prashant Kumar Lal

Author

To,
Augstya, Pushpa,
Akash and Agnes

Contents

1. Makar Sankranti Or Pongal 1
2. Thaipusam 3
3. Vasant Panchami 5
4. Maha Shivaratri 7
5. Hindi New Year 9
6. Holika Dahan 11
7. Holi 13
8. Ugadi, Gudi Padwa And Telugu New Year 15
9. Vaisakhi Or Baisakhi Or Vishu 17
10. Tamil New Year 19
11. Bengali New Year And Bihu 21
12. Ramanavami 23
13. Hanuman Jayanti 25
14. Akshaya Tritiya 27
15. Savitri Pooja 29
16. Puri Rath Yatra 32
17. Guru Purnima 35
18. Nag Panchami 38
19. Varalakshmi Vratam 40
20. Raksha Bandhan 43
21. Shri Krishna Janmashtami 46

22.	Shri Ganesh Chaturthi	49
23.	Vishwakarma Puja	52
24.	Mahalaya Amavasya	55
25.	Navratri Begins	58
26.	Navratri Ends Or Maha Navami	61
27.	Dusshera	64
28.	Sharad Poornima	67
29.	Karva Chauth	70
30.	Dhan Teras	73
31.	Diwali	76
32.	Bhai Dooj	79
33.	Chhath Puja	82
34.	Kartik Purnima	85
35.	Geeta Jayanti	88
36.	Dhanu Sankranti	91
37.	Republic Day	94
38.	Independence Day Of India	97
39.	Gandhi Jayanti	100
40.	Children's Day Of India	102
41.	Teacher's Day In India	105
42.	Honesty	107
43.	Compassion	109
44.	Generosity	111
45.	Respect	114
46.	Responsibility	117
47.	Be True To Yourself	120
48.	Cooperation	123
49.	Courage	126

50. Student's Empowerment 129
51. Gratitude 132
52. Perseverance 135
53. Family 137
54. Justice 139
55. Kindness 142
56. Sharing 145
57. Hard Work 148
58. Moral Compass 151
59. Personal Values 153
60. Building Character 156
61. Environmental Education 159
62. The Value Of Education 162
63. Critical Thinking 165
64. Democratic Education 168
65. Empathy 171
66. Equality 173
67. Health Education 176
68. Moral Development 179
69. Social Education 182
70. Spiritual Education 184
71. Sympathy 186
72. International Day Of Education (Jan 24) 189
73. International Day Of Clean Energy (Jan 26) 192
74. International Day Of Human Fraternity 04 Feb 195
75. World Day Of Social Justice 20 Feb 198
76. World Wildlife Day 03 Mar 201
77. International Women's Day 08 Mar 203

78.	World Water Day 22 Mar	206
79.	International Day Of Zero Waste 30 Mar	209
80.	World Health Day 07 Apr	212
81.	International Mother Earth Day 22 Apr	215
82.	International Day Of Families 15 May	218
83.	World No Tobacco Day 31 May	221
84.	Global Day Of Parents 01 Jun	224
85.	World Environment Day 05 Jun	227
86.	World Day Against Child Labour 12 Jun	229
87.	International Day Of Yoga 21 Jun	232
88.	International Youth Day 12 Aug	235
89.	World Humanitarian Day 19 Aug	238
90.	International Day Of Peace 21 Sep	241
91.	International Day Of Older Persons 01 Oct	244
92.	International Day Of Non-Violence 02 Oct	247
93.	World Habitat Day 07 Oct	250
94.	United Nations Day 24 Oct	253
95.	World Science Day For Peace And Development 10 Nov	256
96.	World Children's Day 20 Nov	259
97.	World Aids Day 01 Dec	262
98.	International Day For The Abolition Of Slavery 02 Dec	265
99.	Human Rights Day 10 Dec	267
100.	World Basketball Day 21 Dec	270

1

Makar Sankranti or Pongal

Good [morning/afternoon/evening] esteemed students, staff, and guests,

Today, we gather to celebrate the vibrant festivals of Makar Sankranti and Pongal, embracing the spirit of harvest, unity, and gratitude. These festivals hold profound cultural significance, and it is essential for us to understand and cherish the traditions they represent.

Makar Sankranti marks the transition of the sun into the zodiac sign of Capricorn, symbolizing the end of winter and the onset of longer, brighter days. Pongal, predominantly celebrated in South India, is a harvest that honours the Sun God and expresses gratitude for a bountiful harvest season.

Now, why are these festivals relevant to us here at [School Name]? Beyond their cultural significance, Makar Sankranti and Pongal teach us valuable lessons about unity, thankfulness, and environmental consciousness. The act of coming together with family, friends, and the community to share joy and food emphasizes the importance of communal bonds and strengthens our sense of belonging. Celebrating these festivals also imparts the lesson of gratitude. As we enjoy the fruits of our labour, it's crucial to recognize the hard work that goes into the cultivation of crops and the contributions of those who make our lives better. Gratitude fosters a positive and appreciative mindset that can significantly enhance our overall well-being.

Moreover, both Makar Sankranti and Pongal emphasize the harmony between humanity and nature. The rituals associated with these festivals encourage us to respect the environment and live in harmony with it. This ecological awareness aligns with our commitment to instil values of responsibility and sustainability in our students.

Now, let's talk about ways to celebrate. Apart from the traditional customs of preparing delicious dishes and flying kites during Makar Sankranti, and cooking the special Pongal dish during Pongal, let's make an effort to celebrate inclusively. Encourage diversity by learning about the various regional customs associated with these festivals. Share your traditions and embrace the rich tapestry of our cultural heritage.

In conclusion, Makar Sankranti and Pongal provide us with an opportunity to reflect on our connection with nature, express gratitude, and celebrate diversity. As we partake in the festivities, let's carry forward the lessons of unity, gratitude, and environmental consciousness into our daily lives. Wishing you all a joyous and meaningful Makar Sankranti and Pongal!

Thank you

Thaipusam

Ladies and gentlemen, students, and esteemed staff,

I stand before you today to shed light on the significance of the Thaipusam festival, a vibrant and culturally rich celebration observed by the Tamil community. Thaipusam commemorates the victory of Lord Murugan over the demon Soorapadman, symbolizing the triumph of good over evil.

During Thaipusam, devotees engage in various religious practices, with the most iconic being the kavadi attam - a ceremonial offering where individuals carry elaborate structures adorned with flowers and peacock feathers. This physical exertion represents the devotee's dedication and determination to overcome obstacles on their spiritual journey.

As we witness this festival, let us draw parallels to our own lives. The resilience and devotion displayed by Thaipusam participants teach us the value of perseverance in the face of challenges. It encourages us to approach our goals with determination, much like the devotees who navigate the challenging kavadi procession.

Furthermore, Thaipusam emphasizes the importance of unity and community support. The collaborative effort involved in organizing and participating in the festivities reflects the strength that comes from standing together. As a school community, let us take inspiration from this and continue fostering an environment of mutual support and understanding.

In conclusion, Thaipusam serves as a reminder of the timeless values of perseverance, devotion, and unity. As we celebrate diversity within our school, let us appreciate and learn from the cultural tapestry that surrounds us. May this festival inspire us to face challenges head-on, build strong bonds within our community, and strive for success with unwavering determination.

Thank you for your attention, and may the spirit of Thaipusam resonate with us all.

3

Vasant Panchami

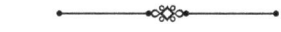

Dear students and esteemed staff,

Namaste! Today, I am delighted to speak about the joyous occasion of Vasant Panchami, a festival that marks the arrival of spring and the onset of the vibrant season.

Vasant Panchami falls on the fifth day of Magha month and holds cultural significance across India. It is a celebration of nature's renewal, as the earth awakens from its winter slumber to embrace the warmth and colours of spring.

The festival is dedicated to Saraswati, the goddess of wisdom, knowledge, and art. We celebrate the embodiment of knowledge on this day, seeking her blessings for academic excellence and artistic endeavours.

One of the distinctive features of Vasant Panchami is the association with yellow colour, symbolizing the vibrancy of life. It is a day when students and teachers alike adorn themselves in yellow attire, filling our surroundings with positivity and energy.

As we immerse ourselves in the festivities, let us not forget the lessons embedded in the celebration. The arrival of spring teaches us about the cyclical nature of life - the inevitable cycle of growth, fruition, and renewal. It reminds us to shed the winter of ignorance and welcome the enlightenment that education brings.

Saraswati Puja, a key ritual during Vasant Panchami, involves offering prayers to the goddess and seeking her blessings. This is a beautiful reminder for all of us to recognize the importance of knowledge in our lives and to be grateful for the opportunities we have to learn and grow.

In the spirit of the festival, let us also reflect on the significance of creativity and artistry. Whether through music, dance, or any form of expression, let our creative endeavours blossom like the flowers of spring.

In conclusion, Vasant Panchami is not just a festival; it is a celebration of life, knowledge, and artistic expression. As we revel in the colours of spring, may we also internalize the essence of this occasion - the pursuit of knowledge, the embrace of creativity, and the continuous cycle of growth and renewal.

I wish each one of you a joyful and enlightening Vasant Panchami. May the blessings of Goddess Saraswati guide us on our academic and creative journeys.

Thank you

4

Maha Shivaratri

Ladies and gentlemen, esteemed faculty, and dear students,

Namaste and a warm welcome to each one of you on this auspicious day of Maha Shivaratri. Today, I would like to shed light on this significant festival that holds great importance in our cultural heritage - Maha Shivaratri.

Maha Shivaratri, or the Great Night of Shiva, is a Hindu festival celebrated in reverence of Lord Shiva. It falls on the 14th night of the dark fortnight in the month of Phalgun, just before the arrival of spring. This festival carries profound spiritual significance and offers valuable lessons for all of us.

Maha Shivaratri symbolizes the overcoming of darkness and ignorance in life. It is a night dedicated to introspection, prayer, and devotion. Lord Shiva, known as the destroyer of evil, teaches us the importance of conquering our inner demons and embracing positive transformation.

On this night, devotees observe a fast and engage in vigil, staying awake to express their devotion to Lord Shiva. Many visit Shiva temples to seek blessings and participate in various rituals, including the Rudra Abhishekam, offering of bilva leaves, and chanting of sacred mantras.

The celebration of Maha Shivaratri imparts essential lessons to our students. It encourages self-discipline through fasting, instils the value of devotion and prayer, and emphasizes the triumph of good over evil. As we partake in the festivities, let us reflect on these teachings and incorporate them into our daily lives.

In conclusion, as we revel in the vibrancy of religious festivals, let us also recognize the spiritual significance of Maha Shivaratri. May this festival inspire us to overcome challenges, cultivate inner strength, and foster a sense of unity and devotion in our school community.

Thank you, and may the blessings of Lord Shiva be with us all.

5

Hindi New Year

Esteemed faculty, and dear students,

Namaskar!

Today, as we gather to celebrate the Hindi New Year, let us delve into the significance of this auspicious occasion and the rich traditions associated with it.

The Hindi New Year, also known as "Nav Varsh" or "Vikram Samvat," marks the beginning of a new lunar calendar. It's a time for reflection, renewal, and the embrace of fresh opportunities. This occasion is not just about turning a new leaf in our calendars; it's about fostering a spirit of optimism and embracing the cultural heritage that binds us together.

As we celebrate, let us take a moment to reflect on the lessons embedded in this festive occasion. The Hindi New Year teaches us the importance of resilience and adaptation to change. Just as the moon waxes and wanes, life presents us with cycles of ups and downs. This celebration encourages us to face challenges with grace and welcome new beginnings with open hearts.

The festivities surrounding the Hindi New Year are vibrant and diverse. Families come together to clean and decorate their homes, symbolizing the cleansing of the past and making way for a brighter future. The exchange of sweets and warm wishes fosters a sense of community and unity among us.

Moreover, this occasion is an excellent opportunity to emphasize the importance of our mother tongue, Hindi. It is the thread that weaves through the fabric of our cultural identity. Let us cherish and preserve our language, understanding that it connects us to our roots and helps us communicate with authenticity.

In conclusion, the Hindi New Year is not just a date on the calendar; it is a celebration of our shared history, our language, and the resilience that defines our journey. As we embark on this new year, let us carry forward the lessons learned, embrace change, and foster a sense of unity within our school community.

Thank you, and I wish each one of you a joyous and prosperous Hindi New Year! Jai Hind!

6

Holika Dahan

Ladies and gentlemen, esteemed students, and respected staff,

I stand before you today to shed light on the significance of Holika Dahan, a festival deeply rooted in our cultural heritage. Holika Dahan, celebrated on the eve of Holi, holds great importance in the Hindu calendar.

This festival symbolizes the victory of good over evil, a theme resonant with the values we instil in our students here at our esteemed institution. As we gather around the sacred fire, let us reflect on the lessons embedded in this age-old tradition.

Holika Dahan is not merely about the ritualistic bonfire; it's a symbolic act representing the triumph of virtue. The story of Prahlad and Holika serves as a timeless reminder that righteousness prevails over malevolence. In our academic journey, it's crucial for us to choose the path of integrity and knowledge, defeating ignorance and prejudice.

The vibrant colours of Holi, which follows Holika Dahan, teach us the beauty of unity in diversity. This festival transcends barriers, bringing people together from all walks of life. Similarly, within our school community, let us celebrate our differences, appreciating the unique talents and perspectives each individual contributes.

As we witness the flames engulfing the effigy of Holika, let it ignite the flame of determination within us to overcome obstacles and challenges. Just as Prahlad emerged unscathed from the fire, let us emerge stronger and resilient in the face of adversities.

In conclusion, Holika Dahan is not just a ritual but a celebration of virtue, unity, and resilience. As we partake in the festivities, let's internalize these values and carry them forward in our academic pursuits and daily lives.

Thank you, and may the spirit of Holika Dahan inspire us all.

7

Holi

Ladies and gentlemen, esteemed students and staff,

Good [morning/afternoon],

I stand before you today to celebrate the vibrant festival of Holi, a time-honoured tradition that unites us in a colourful tapestry of joy and togetherness. Holi, also known as the Festival of Colours, holds immense cultural significance, symbolizing the triumph of good over evil and the arrival of spring.

As we prepare to immerse ourselves in the festivities, it's essential to understand the deeper lessons embedded in this colourful celebration. Holi teaches us the importance of breaking down barriers and embracing diversity. Just as different colours come together to create a beautiful spectrum, we, too, must appreciate and respect the uniqueness each individual brings to our school community.

The tradition of throwing vibrant powders and water during Holi signifies the cleansing of the soul and renewal of relationships. It serves as a reminder to let go of grudges and foster a spirit of forgiveness and reconciliation within our school community. As we engage in the playful exchange of colours, let us also reflect on the need for harmony and understanding among us.

Furthermore, Holi underscores the concept of equality. The festival transcends social boundaries, bringing people from all walks of life together in a spirit of camaraderie. Let us carry this message into our daily lives, treating each other with kindness and respect, irrespective of our differences.

In the spirit of Holi, I encourage all of you to partake in the festivities responsibly. Ensure that the celebrations are inclusive, considering the comfort and preferences of everyone involved. Let us cherish the joyous moments, creating memories that bind us together in a spirit of unity.

As we revel in the colours of Holi, may we also absorb the invaluable lessons it imparts - the significance of diversity, the power of forgiveness, and the beauty of unity. Let this celebration be a reflection of the harmonious community we aspire to create within our school.

Thank you, and may this Holi bring warmth, happiness, and a renewed sense of togetherness to each one of you.

8

Ugadi, Gudi Padwa and Telugu New Year

Ladies and Gentlemen, esteemed faculty, and cherished students,

As we gather here today, I extend my warmest greetings on the auspicious occasion of Ugadi, Gudi Padwa, and Telugu New Year. This celebration marks not only the changing of the calendar but also symbolizes the renewal of spirit and the beginning of new possibilities.

Ugadi, with its vibrant festivities, teaches us the significance of embracing change with enthusiasm. Just as the neem and jaggery mixture - symbolic of life's bitter and sweet experiences - herald the new year, let us approach each challenge and success with resilience and optimism.

This day encourages us to reflect on the past, appreciate the present, and look forward to the future. As an educational community, let us celebrate the diverse talents and perspectives that make our school vibrant and dynamic.

Ways to celebrate this occasion could include cultural programs, traditional decorations, and sharing festive meals. By participating in these activities, we strengthen our bonds and foster a sense of unity among students and staff.

Ugadi also imparts valuable lessons about the cycles of life. Just as nature undergoes transformations, so do our lives. Let us embrace growth, learning, and change, recognizing that every experience contributes to our personal and collective evolution.

In conclusion, as we embark on this new year, let us carry the spirit of Ugadi with us. May it inspire us to approach challenges with resilience, cherish our achievements, and build a supportive and united community within our school.

Thank you for your attention, and I wish each and every one of you a joyous and prosperous Ugadi, Gudi Padwa, and Telugu New Year.

9

Vaisakhi or Baisakhi or Vishu

Ladies and gentlemen, esteemed students and dedicated staff,

I stand before you today to celebrate the vibrant festival of Vaishakhi, also known as Baishakhi or Vishu, which holds significant cultural and historical importance in various parts of our country.

Vaishakhi marks the beginning of the traditional solar year and is celebrated with enthusiasm and fervour. Its historical roots are deeply embedded in our rich cultural tapestry, tracing back to agricultural traditions, harvest celebrations, and the formation of Sikhism.

In the agricultural context, Vaishakhi signifies the joy of a bountiful harvest, symbolizing prosperity and abundance. It serves as a reminder of our connection to the land and the importance of agricultural practices in our society.

Moreover, Vaishakhi holds great religious significance for the Sikh community, as it commemorates the day of the establishment of the Khalsa Panth by Guru Gobind Singh Ji in 1699. This event marked a turning point in Sikh history, emphasizing the values of courage, equality, and justice.

As we celebrate Vaishakhi, let us embrace the spirit of unity and diversity. It is an occasion to appreciate the multicultural fabric of our school community, where individuals from various backgrounds come together to learn, grow, and share their unique traditions.

To celebrate Vaishakhi, consider organizing cultural events, traditional performances, and educational activities that highlight the festival's significance. Encourage students to share their family traditions related to Vaishakhi, fostering a sense of pride in their cultural heritage.

In conclusion, let this Vaishakhi be a time of reflection, celebration, and learning. May it inspire us to appreciate the diverse tapestry of our community and reinforce the values of unity, respect, and understanding.

Wishing you all a joyous and meaningful Vaishakhi celebration!

10

Tamil New Year

Ladies and gentlemen, esteemed students and dedicated staff,

I stand before you today to celebrate and honour the rich cultural tapestry that is Tamil New Year. This auspicious occasion holds deep historical significance, rooted in the traditions and customs that have shaped the Tamil community for centuries.

Tamil New Year, also known as Puthandu, marks the beginning of the Tamil calendar. Its origins can be traced back to ancient times when our ancestors observed the celestial movements and agricultural cycles. This day not only symbolizes a fresh start but also serves as a reminder of the cultural resilience that has endured through time.

As we embark on this new year, let us reflect on the teachings embedded in our traditions. The rituals associated with Tamil New Year are not merely customs but convey profound lessons. The act of cleaning our homes symbolizes the importance of purifying our minds and hearts, fostering a sense of inner renewal.

The traditional feast prepared during this time not only tantalizes our taste buds but also signifies the abundance of life's blessings. Sharing these meals with family and neighbours underscores the spirit of unity and togetherness that defines our community.

In the spirit of festivity, the Kolam patterns drawn at our thresholds represent the artistry and precision that each individual brings to the collective canvas of our society. Each stroke of the Kolam is a testament to the beauty that emerges when we contribute our unique talents to the community.

While we revel in the joyous festivities, let us not forget the importance of preserving our cultural heritage. The Tamil New Year serves as a reminder to cherish and pass down our customs to future generations, ensuring that the flame of our tradition continues to burn brightly.

As we celebrate this occasion, let us also embrace the virtues of patience, resilience, and gratitude. The resilience of the Tamil community throughout history has shown that adversity can be overcome through unity and determination.

In conclusion, let Tamil New Year be a time of reflection, celebration, and commitment to our cultural roots. May the lessons embedded in our traditions guide us towards a harmonious and prosperous future. Wishing you all a joyous and fulfilling Tamil New Year!

11

Bengali New Year and Bihu

Dear Students, Esteemed Staff, and Respected Guests,

I stand before you today with immense joy and warmth as we come together to celebrate the Bengali New Year, also known as Pohela Boishakh, and Bihu. These festivals hold great significance, not just as occasions to mark the beginning of the new year, but as celebrations deeply rooted in our cultural heritage.

Pohela Boishakh, with its vibrant festivities and cultural richness, represents the spirit of renewal and unity. As we witness the magnificent processions, traditional dances, and the creation of alpana, let us remember that these activities are not just rituals but expressions of our shared identity and values.

This festival teaches us the importance of cultural preservation and passing down traditions to the younger generations. It's a reminder that our roots provide nourishment, and by understanding and respecting our heritage, we contribute to the richness of our collective tapestry.

Similarly, Bihu, celebrated with much fervour in Assam, marks the Assamese New Year. The Bihu dance, with its lively and energetic movements, reflects the rhythm of life in Assam. It symbolizes the joy of living in harmony with nature and the agricultural cycles. As a community, let us learn from this connection with nature and foster a sense of environmental responsibility.

The lessons embedded in these celebrations are profound. They remind us to appreciate the cyclical nature of life, the importance of unity in diversity, and the need to cultivate a harmonious relationship with the world around us. In embracing our cultural roots, we find strength, resilience, and a sense of belonging.

As a school community, let us celebrate these festivals with enthusiasm, participation, and respect. Through cultural exchanges and shared experiences, we can foster a deeper understanding and appreciation for the diversity within our student body and staff.

In conclusion, Pohela Boishakh and Bihu invite us to reflect on our shared heritage, values, and the interconnectedness of our lives. May this new year bring prosperity, joy, and a renewed sense of purpose to each one of us.

Thank you for your attention, and I wish you all a joyous and culturally enriching celebration of the Bengali New Year and Bihu. Shubho Noboborsho! Rongali Bihu Rongali Bihu Bihuwanu!

12

Ramanavami

Dear Students, Esteemed Staff, and Honoured Guests,

Today, I address you to illuminate the significance of Ramanavami, a festival that encapsulates profound cultural and spiritual meanings in our heritage.

Ramanavami, celebrated on the birthday of Lord Rama, stands as a testament to the virtues of righteousness, duty, and devotion. Lord Rama, the seventh avatar of Lord Vishnu, exemplifies the ideals of an ideal ruler, son, and husband.

The importance of Ramanavami lies not only in its religious context but also in the moral and ethical values it symbolizes. Lord Rama's life teaches us about the importance of adhering to principles, even in the face of adversity. His unwavering commitment to Dharma serves as a guiding light, encouraging us to uphold righteousness in our own lives.

Ways to celebrate Ramanavami often include recitation of Rama Katha, prayers, and bhajans. These rituals are not mere acts of devotion but opportunities for self-reflection and spiritual growth. As a school community, we can integrate these practices into our lives, fostering an environment that values morality and ethical conduct.

The lessons embedded in Ramanavami are timeless. Lord Rama's journey teaches us about the complexities of life, the importance of fulfilling our responsibilities, and the strength derived from unwavering faith and integrity.

Ramanavami also underscores the significance of familial relationships and the responsibilities that come with them. Lord Rama's devotion to his parents and commitment to his role as a son serve as an inspiration for us to honour and cherish our familial bonds.

In celebrating Ramanavami, let us not merely partake in rituals but internalize the values it represents. Strive for moral uprightness, fulfil responsibilities with dedication, and cultivate a sense of duty towards society. Let the spirit of Ramanavami guide us towards becoming individuals of character and integrity.

In conclusion, I urge each one of you to engage in the celebration of Ramanavami with reverence and introspection. May this festival inspire us to lead lives guided by principles, virtue, and a deep sense of duty.

Thank you for your attention, and I wish you all a spiritually enriching and morally uplifting Ramanavami celebration. May the teachings of Lord Rama illuminate our paths and inspire positive transformation in our lives.

13

Hanuman Jayanti

Ladies and gentlemen, esteemed faculty, and dear students,

Namaste! Today, as we gather to celebrate Hanuman Jayanti, we delve into a rich tapestry of history, significance, and valuable lessons from the life of Lord Hanuman.

Hanuman Jayanti marks the birth of Lord Hanuman, a divine figure revered for his unwavering devotion, strength, and selfless service. His tale resonates with timeless lessons that extend beyond religious boundaries.

In the Ramayana, we find Hanuman's exemplary dedication to Lord Rama. His courage, humility, and loyalty serve as a beacon for us all. Hanuman's boundless devotion teaches us the power of faith and the strength that emanates from unwavering commitment.

The celebration of Hanuman Jayanti isn't merely a ritual; it's an opportunity for introspection. As we honour Lord

Hanuman, let us reflect on the virtues he embodies - resilience, humility, and selflessness. These virtues are the pillars upon which a strong character is built.

Just as Hanuman leaped across the ocean to fulfil his mission, let us strive to overcome obstacles in our lives with determination and perseverance. Hanuman's steadfastness in the face of challenges inspires us to approach difficulties with a resilient spirit.

Hanuman Jayanti is a time to celebrate the triumph of good over evil. As we engage in festivities, let us also reflect on the triumphs of virtue in our own lives. Embracing righteousness and compassion, we contribute to a harmonious community and a better world.

The rituals associated with Hanuman Jayanti, such as reading the Ramayana and chanting hymns, provide us with an opportunity for spiritual growth and self-discovery. Through these practices, we can cultivate inner strength and foster a sense of inner peace.

In conclusion, let Hanuman Jayanti serve as a reminder of the timeless wisdom encapsulated in Lord Hanuman's life. As we celebrate today, may we carry forward the lessons of dedication, resilience, and selflessness into our daily lives. May the spirit of Hanuman inspire us all to be better individuals, fostering a positive environment within our school and beyond.

Thank you, and may the blessings of Lord Hanuman be with each one of us. Jai Hanuman!

14

Akshaya Tritiya

Ladies and gentlemen, esteemed faculty, and cherished students,

I stand before you today to share insights on a significant and auspicious occasion in our cultural calendar - Akshaya Tritiya. This day holds profound importance in the tapestry of our traditions, and understanding its history and embracing meaningful celebrations can enrich our lives.

Akshaya Tritiya, also known as Akti or Akha Teej, falls on the third lunar day of the bright half of Vaishakha month. Its roots are embedded in Hindu mythology, with references in the epic Mahabharata. Legend has it that on this day, Lord Parashurama, the sixth avatar of Lord Vishnu, was born. It is also believed to be the day when Lord Ganesha started scribing the epic Mahabharata to Ved Vyasa.

The term "Akshaya" means eternal or everlasting, and Tritiya refers to the third lunar day. Together, they symbolize a day of unending prosperity and good fortune. It's considered an opportune time to initiate new ventures, make investments, and embark on significant life endeavours.

As we navigate through the pages of history, we uncover the tradition of purchasing gold on Akshaya Tritiya. Gold, regarded as a symbol of wealth and prosperity, is believed to bring continuous success and good fortune. Many families consider buying gold on this day, creating a tradition that reflects not only financial prudence but also cultural reverence.

Now, let us ponder upon the ways we can celebrate Akshaya Tritiya meaningfully. Beyond the material aspects, this day offers a chance for spiritual reflection and community engagement. Encourage acts of charity, kindness, and compassion. Engage in activities that promote sustainability and the well-being of our environment.

Consider organizing cultural programs or workshops that delve into the rich history and significance of Akshaya Tritiya. This fosters a sense of unity among students, allowing them to appreciate the cultural diversity that enriches our school community.

In conclusion, Akshaya Tritiya is not merely a day for material gains but an opportunity to align ourselves with timeless values and cultural richness. Embrace the spirit of this auspicious occasion with a mindful celebration that extends beyond individual prosperity to encompass the collective well-being of our school community.

May this Akshaya Tritiya bring boundless blessings, prosperity, and joy to each one of you.

Thank you

15

Savitri Pooja

Ladies and gentlemen, esteemed faculty, and dear students,

I stand before you today to shed light on a significant cultural celebration, Savitri Pooja. This auspicious occasion holds deep roots in our traditions and offers valuable lessons that resonate through generations.

Savitri Pooja, also known as Vat Savitri Vrat, traces its origins to ancient Hindu mythology. It commemorates the exemplary devotion and courage of Savitri, a woman whose unwavering dedication saved her husband, Satyavan, from the clutches of death. Her resilience and commitment have turned this day into a symbol of marital bliss and the strength of love.

As we celebrate Savitri Pooja, it is essential to recognize the importance of preserving and passing on these cultural practices to the younger generation. Our rich heritage serves as a foundation for understanding the values that bind our society together. By participating in rituals like Savitri Pooja, we connect with our roots and appreciate the profound wisdom embedded in our traditions.

The ways of celebrating Savitri Pooja vary across regions, but common elements include fasting, prayers, and tying threads around banyan trees. These rituals symbolize devotion, sacrifice, and the eternal bond between spouses. By partaking in these customs, we not only honour our cultural heritage but also strengthen the bonds within our community.

Moreover, the lessons derived from Savitri Pooja extend beyond the realm of marital devotion. Savitri's courage teaches us the power of resilience in the face of adversity. It reminds us that determination and unwavering faith can overcome seemingly insurmountable challenges. These values are pertinent not only in our personal lives but also in the pursuit of academic and professional excellence.

In today's fast-paced world, where values sometimes take a back seat, Savitri Pooja serves as a beacon, guiding us towards a life grounded in principles. As students and educators, let us reflect on the dedication displayed by Savitri and strive to approach our academic pursuits with a similar passion and commitment.

In conclusion, Savitri Pooja is not merely a ritual; it is a celebration of love, devotion, and resilience. As we observe this day, let us embrace the cultural richness it brings, draw inspiration from the timeless tale of Savitri, and apply the lessons learned in our daily lives. May this celebration foster unity, understanding, and a deep appreciation for the values that shape our identity.

Thank you, and may this Savitri Pooja bring blessings and wisdom to each one of us.

16

Puri Rath Yatra

Dear Students, Esteemed Staff, and Honoured Guests,

I am delighted to stand before you today to shed light on the significance of one of the most revered festivals in our culture - the Puri Rath Yatra. This grand celebration not only holds immense religious importance but also offers valuable lessons for us all.

The Rath Yatra, or Chariot Festival, is an occasion deeply rooted in our traditions. It commemorates Lord Jagannath's annual journey to his aunt's temple, accompanied by his siblings Balabhadra and Subhadra. The majestic chariots, the pulling of which involves the collective strength of devotees, symbolize the unity and devotion that bind our community together.

The grandeur of the Rath Yatra teaches us the importance of shared faith and collective effort. Just as devotees come together to pull the massive chariots, let us appreciate the strength that unity brings to our school community. By working together, we can overcome challenges, support one another, and achieve shared goals.

Celebrating Rath Yatra is not merely a ritual; it is a demonstration of our commitment to traditions and spirituality. As a school, we can embody this spirit by fostering an environment where respect for diverse beliefs is upheld. Understanding and appreciating each other's traditions contribute to a harmonious and inclusive community.

The Rath Yatra also imparts the lesson of humility. Regardless of caste, creed, or social status, everyone participates in the procession as equals. This humility is a valuable trait for us to cultivate in our lives, reminding us that true strength lies not in our individual achievements but in our ability to stand together with humility and empathy.

As we celebrate this festival, let us explore ways to integrate its lessons into our daily lives. Encourage open-mindedness, embrace diversity, and work collectively towards common objectives. Let the spirit of Rath Yatra inspire us to approach challenges with determination, humility, and a sense of shared purpose.

In conclusion, I invite each one of you to actively participate in the celebrations of Puri Rath Yatra. Let us not only observe the rituals but also internalize the lessons it offers. May this festival strengthen our bonds, deepen our understanding of cultural diversity, and guide us towards a more compassionate and united school community.

Thank you for your attention, and I wish you all a joyous and spiritually enriching Puri Rath Yatra celebration. Jai Jagannath!

17

Guru Purnima

Dear Students, Respected Staff, and Honoured Guests,

Today, we gather with reverence and gratitude to celebrate Guru Purnima, a day that holds profound significance in our cultural and spiritual heritage. This occasion allows us to reflect on the role of teachers and mentors in shaping our lives.

Guru Purnima is a day dedicated to expressing gratitude to our teachers, mentors, and guides. It is celebrated on the full moon day of the Hindu month of Ashadha, honouring the birth anniversary of the great sage Vyasa. Vyasa, revered for his role in compiling the Vedas and composing the Mahabharata, symbolizes the eternal bond between a teacher and a disciple.

The importance of Guru Purnima lies in acknowledging the pivotal role that teachers play in our lives. They are not just conveyors of knowledge but architects of character, instilling values and wisdom that go beyond textbooks. As a school community, let us take this opportunity to express our gratitude to the dedicated educators who inspire, guide, and mould the future of our students.

Ways to celebrate Guru Purnima can include special prayers, cultural programs, and expressions of gratitude. Students may choose to honour their teachers through cards, messages, or small tokens of appreciation, recognizing the invaluable impact they have on their academic and personal development.

The lessons embedded in Guru Purnima extend beyond the ceremonial aspects. It teaches us the importance of lifelong learning, humility, and the transformative power of knowledge. Just as a river constantly flows and enriches the land it touches, knowledge should be shared selflessly, creating a ripple effect that positively influences society.

Guru Purnima encourages us to be receptive to guidance, acknowledging that learning is a continuous process. It is a reminder that education goes beyond the confines of the classroom; it is a journey of self-discovery and enlightenment facilitated by the wisdom of our teachers.

In conclusion, let us celebrate Guru Purnima with sincerity and gratitude. May this occasion serve as a reminder of the profound impact teachers have on our lives and inspire us to approach learning with humility and openness. As we express our gratitude, let us also commit to being lifelong learners, continuously seeking knowledge and wisdom.

Thank you for your attention, and I wish you all a reflective and joyous Guru Purnima celebration. May the light of knowledge guide us all on our paths of learning and growth.

18

Nag Panchami

Dear Students, Esteemed Staff, and Respected Guests,

Today, I stand before you to shed light on the significance of Nag Panchami, a festival that holds deep cultural and spiritual importance in our traditions.

Nag Panchami is observed on the fifth day of the bright half of the lunar month of Shravan. Its roots lie in ancient mythology, with serpents or Nagas playing a prominent role. In Hindu mythology, snakes are associated with divine energy, protection, and fertility.

The importance of Nag Panchami extends beyond its religious connotations. It serves as a reminder of our interconnectedness with nature and the creatures that share our world. Snakes, often misunderstood and feared, are revered on this day as symbols of cosmic energy and guardianship.

Celebrating Nag Panchami involves rituals such as snake worship, where images of snakes are adorned and offerings are made. This ritual is not merely a tradition but a way to express our gratitude and respect for the natural world around us. As a school community, we can integrate this spirit by fostering an appreciation for the environment and its diverse inhabitants.

The lessons embedded in Nag Panchami are profound. Snakes, despite their fearsome reputation, are not aggressive unless provoked. This teaches us the importance of understanding and respecting the natural world, approaching it with a sense of balance and harmony.

Nag Panchami also emphasizes the need for protection and preservation of endangered species. As custodians of our planet's biodiversity, we have a responsibility to ensure the well-being of all living beings, promoting ecological balance and coexistence.

In celebrating Nag Panchami, let us not just perform rituals but internalize the values it represents. Cultivate empathy, understanding, and a sense of responsibility towards the environment. Recognize the interconnectedness of all life forms, and strive to create a community that values and respects the natural world.

In conclusion, I invite each one of you to engage in the spirit of Nag Panchami with reverence and mindfulness. May this festival inspire us to be stewards of the environment, fostering a sense of responsibility towards the creatures we share this planet with.

Thank you for your attention, and I wish you all a meaningful and environmentally conscious Nag Panchami celebration. May our actions reflect our commitment to preserving the delicate balance of nature.

19

Varalakshmi Vratam

Respected faculty, dear students, and esteemed guests,

I am honoured to address you today as we gather to delve into the significance and traditions surrounding Varalakshmi Vratam, a festival that holds great importance in our cultural tapestry.

Varalakshmi Vratam, also known as Varalakshmi Puja, is a celebration dedicated to the goddess Lakshmi, the embodiment of wealth, prosperity, and auspiciousness. This festival finds its roots in the Hindu tradition, particularly in South India, and is observed with fervour and devotion by families seeking the blessings of the divine goddess.

The history of Varalakshmi Vratam is intertwined with a beautiful narrative. Legend has it that Goddess Parvati, in the form of Varalakshmi, appeared before a devoted woman named Charumati and granted her the boon of fulfilment of wishes. Inspired by this story, Varalakshmi Vratam is observed by married women seeking the well-being and prosperity of their families. It is believed that performing the rituals with sincerity and devotion during this day can bestow blessings, wealth, and success.

Now, let's explore the ways in which this festival is traditionally celebrated. Varalakshmi Vratam typically involves a meticulous puja, where an idol or an image of Goddess Lakshmi is adorned with flowers, silk, and jewellery. Women perform special prayers, offer naivedyam (sacred food), and tie sacred threads, all with the hope of invoking the goddess's divine presence.

The act of observing a strict fast on this day is another customary practice, symbolizing discipline and self-control. As we partake in these rituals, it is crucial to understand that the essence lies not just in the outward ceremonies but in the depth of devotion and purity of heart with which they are performed.

Celebrating Varalakshmi Vratam is an opportunity for us to connect with our spiritual roots, fostering a sense of unity and cultural identity. It serves as a reminder of the values that guide our lives, emphasizing the significance of gratitude, humility, and the pursuit of noble virtues.

For our students, Varalakshmi Vratam provides a valuable lesson in cultural diversity and respect for traditions. By participating in the festivities, we learn to appreciate the customs that contribute to the rich mosaic of our society. It is a day that transcends religious boundaries, inviting everyone to come together and celebrate the universal ideals of prosperity and well-being.

In conclusion, Varalakshmi Vratam is not just a religious observance; it is a cultural celebration that resonates with the spirit of unity, devotion, and prosperity. As we embark on the festivities, let us do so with a heart full of reverence, embracing the teachings that this day imparts. May the blessings of Goddess Lakshmi shower upon us all, nurturing a harmonious and prosperous community.

Thank you, and may this Varalakshmi Vratam bring joy and fulfilment to each one of you.

20

Raksha Bandhan

Respected faculty, dear students, and honoured guests,

Today, I stand before you to delve into the cultural significance of a beautiful celebration that binds the threads of love and protection - Raksha Bandhan. As we explore the importance, history, ways to celebrate, and the inherent lessons of this occasion, let us reflect on the profound meaning it holds for each one of us.

Raksha Bandhan, also known as the "bond of protection," is a timeless celebration of the unique and sacred relationship between siblings. This day signifies the unwavering bond of love and commitment that exists between a brother and a sister. The history of Raksha Bandhan is rooted in tales of bravery, sacrifice, and the commitment to safeguard one another.

One of the most iconic legends associated with Raksha Bandhan is the story of Queen Karnavati and Emperor Humayun. Facing imminent danger, Queen Karnavati sent a Rakhi to Humayun, seeking his protection. Touched by the bond of love, Humayun rushed to her aid, emphasizing the symbolic importance of the Rakhi as a thread of protection.

The ways to celebrate Raksha Bandhan are diverse, but they all revolve around a simple yet powerful ritual – the tying of the Rakhi. Sisters adorn their brothers' wrists with intricately designed threads, signifying their love, prayers, and the promise of protection. In return, brothers offer gifts and a pledge to safeguard their sisters in times of need.

Beyond the threads and gifts, Raksha Bandhan imparts valuable lessons. It teaches us the significance of relationships, the importance of mutual support, and the commitment to stand by our loved ones through thick and thin. The festival underscores the idea that the strength of familial bonds forms a foundation for personal growth and societal harmony.

As we celebrate Raksha Bandhan within our school community, let us embrace the diversity it brings. The occasion is not confined to a particular region or religion; rather, it transcends cultural boundaries, symbolizing the universal theme of love and protection. It encourages us to appreciate and respect the diverse traditions that contribute to the vibrant mosaic of our society.

In conclusion, Raksha Bandhan is not just a festival; it is a celebration of love, trust, and the unbreakable ties that bind us together. As we exchange Rakhis and promises, let us internalize the profound lessons it imparts and foster a sense of unity and support within our school community.

Thank you, and may this Raksha Bandhan bring joy, love, and enduring bonds to each one of you.

21

Shri Krishna Janmashtami

Respected faculty, dear students, and esteemed guests,

Today, I am honoured to address you on the occasion of Shri Krishna Janmashtami, a festival that holds profound significance in our cultural and spiritual heritage. As we come together to celebrate the birth of Lord Krishna, let us explore the importance, history, ways to celebrate, and the timeless lessons embedded in this joyous occasion.

Shri Krishna Janmashtami marks the birth of Lord Krishna, the eighth incarnation of Lord Vishnu, revered for his wisdom, playfulness, and divine teachings. The historical roots of this festival can be traced back to the Dvapara Yuga, an era when Lord Krishna took human form to guide humanity on the path of righteousness.

One of the most revered stories associated with Janmashtami is the midnight birth of Lord Krishna in Mathura, where he emerged in a prison cell to Devaki and Vasudeva. The events surrounding his birth, such as the divine exchange with Yashoda and the iconic tale of the butter theft, contribute to the rich tapestry of Janmashtami.

Celebrating Janmashtami involves various customs and rituals. Devotees observe fasts, engage in devotional singing and dancing known as 'Raas Leela,' and participate in processions and prayer sessions at temples. The highlight of the celebration is the 'Dahi Handi' tradition, symbolizing the mischievous acts of young Krishna, who would steal butter from hanging pots. This event brings communities together, fostering a sense of camaraderie and joy.

Beyond the festivity, Janmashtami imparts timeless lessons. Lord Krishna's teachings, encapsulated in the Bhagavad Gita, offer profound insights into duty, righteousness, and the path to spiritual enlightenment. The essence of selfless action, detachment, and devotion to a higher purpose resonates through Krishna's wisdom, providing a guiding light for individuals navigating the complexities of life.

As we celebrate Janmashtami within our school community, let us embrace the diversity it brings. The occasion transcends cultural and regional boundaries, symbolizing universal values that resonate with people of different backgrounds. It encourages us to appreciate and respect the spiritual richness that contributes to the vibrant tapestry of our society.

In conclusion, Shri Krishna Janmashtami is not merely a celebration; it is a spiritual journey that invites us to reflect on the teachings of Lord Krishna. As we immerse ourselves in the festivities, let us internalize the profound lessons he imparts and strive to embody the virtues of righteousness, devotion, and selfless action in our lives.

Thank you, and may this Janmashtami bring joy, wisdom, and spiritual enlightenment to each one of you.

22

Shri Ganesh Chaturthi

Respected faculty, dear students, and esteemed guests,

I am honoured to address you today on the auspicious occasion of Shri Ganesh Chaturthi, a celebration that holds great significance in our cultural and spiritual heritage. As we come together to observe the birth of Lord Ganesha, let us explore the history, importance, ways to celebrate, and the valuable lessons embedded in this joyous festival.

Shri Ganesh Chaturthi marks the birth of Lord Ganesha, the elephant-headed deity revered as the remover of obstacles and the patron of intellect and wisdom. The historical roots of this festival date back to ancient scriptures, where Ganesha is portrayed as a symbol of good fortune, knowledge, and the harbinger of success in endeavours.

The story of Ganesha's creation by Goddess Parvati, his role as a guardian of entrances, and the iconic episode of winning a race around the world against Lord Kartikeya emphasize the importance of intellect, humility, and determination in overcoming challenges.

The ways to celebrate Ganesh Chaturthi are diverse and vibrant. Devotees install Ganesha idols in their homes and community pandals, embarking on a ten-day celebration filled with prayers, rituals, and cultural events. The installation of the idol is accompanied by chanting of sacred hymns, offering of sweets, and engaging in devotional songs. On the final day, the immersion of the idol, known as Visarjan, symbolizes the cycle of creation and dissolution, reminding us of the impermanence of life.

Beyond the festivities, Ganesh Chaturthi imparts valuable lessons. Lord Ganesha, known for his large ears symbolizing the importance of listening, teaches us the significance of acquiring knowledge and wisdom. His elephant head represents memory and intelligence, guiding us to approach challenges with intellect and perseverance.

As we celebrate Ganesh Chaturthi within our school community, let us embrace the diversity it brings. The occasion transcends cultural and regional boundaries, symbolizing universal values of wisdom, humility, and the triumph of good over obstacles. It encourages us to appreciate and respect the spiritual richness that contributes to the vibrant tapestry of our society.

In conclusion, Shri Ganesh Chaturthi is not just a celebration; it is a spiritual journey that invites us to reflect on the teachings of Lord Ganesha. As we immerse ourselves in the festivities, let us internalize the profound lessons he imparts and strive to embody the virtues of knowledge, humility, and resilience in our lives.

Thank you, and may this Ganesh Chaturthi bring joy, wisdom, and the removal of obstacles to each one of you.

Vishwakarma Puja

Respected faculty, dear students, and honoured guests,

I stand before you today to share insights into a celebration that holds great significance in our cultural tapestry - Vishwakarma Puja. As we explore the history, importance, ways to celebrate, and the lessons inherent in this occasion, let us delve into the spirit of craftsmanship and innovation that Vishwakarma Puja embodies.

Vishwakarma Puja is dedicated to Lord Vishwakarma, the divine architect and craftsman of the gods in Hindu mythology. This day is observed to honour the supreme creator, the master craftsman who is believed to have built the celestial weapons and vehicles for gods. The history of Vishwakarma Puja can be traced back to ancient scriptures where the divine architect is revered for his exceptional skills and contributions to the world of craftsmanship.

The importance of Vishwakarma Puja lies in its recognition of the vital role played by artisans, craftsmen, and all those involved in creative endeavours. It is a day to celebrate the spirit of innovation, hard work, and dedication that goes into crafting objects, buildings, and technologies that shape our world.

Ways to celebrate Vishwakarma Puja vary across regions, but common elements include the consecration of tools and machinery, traditional rituals, and the creation of colourful rangolis. Industries, workshops, and factories often shut down on this day, allowing workers and craftsmen to participate in the festivities. The puja is not only about worship but also about expressing gratitude for the skills that contribute to the progress and development of society.

Beyond the celebrations, Vishwakarma Puja imparts valuable lessons. It emphasizes the importance of recognizing and appreciating the efforts of those involved in craftsmanship and innovation. Lord Vishwakarma's dedication to his craft serves as an inspiration, urging us to take pride in our work, regardless of its nature. It encourages us to approach our tasks with a sense of responsibility and creativity, fostering a spirit of continuous improvement.

As we celebrate Vishwakarma Puja within our school community, let us embrace the diversity it brings. The occasion transcends cultural and regional boundaries, symbolizing the universal values of craftsmanship and innovation. It encourages us to appreciate and respect the varied skills and talents that contribute to the vibrant tapestry of our society.

In conclusion, Vishwakarma Puja is not just a ritual; it is a celebration of creativity, dedication, and the spirit of craftsmanship. As we immerse ourselves in the festivities, let us internalize the profound lessons it imparts and strive to embody the virtues of innovation, hard work, and continuous improvement in our lives.

Thank you, and may this Vishwakarma Puja bring inspiration, creativity, and success to each one of you.

24

Mahalaya Amavasya

Respected faculty, dear students, and esteemed guests,

Today, I address you on the occasion of Mahalaya Amavasya, a significant and spiritually enriching day in our cultural calendar. As we come together to understand the importance, history, ways to celebrate, and the lessons embedded in this sacred day, let us explore the profound significance it holds for our community.

Mahalaya Amavasya marks the beginning of Devi Paksha and is observed with reverence and devotion across various regions in India. The significance of this day lies in its connection to the advent of Goddess Durga, the divine embodiment of power, strength, and compassion. Mahalaya, which falls on the last day of the dark fortnight, is considered the day when the souls of our ancestors descend to the earthly realm.

The history of Mahalaya Amavasya is deeply rooted in Hindu mythology. It is believed that Lord Rama, seeking the blessings of Goddess Durga before embarking on his battle against Ravana, performed a ritual known as "Tarpan" on this day to honour his ancestors. This tradition of paying homage to our forefathers continues today as families perform rituals and prayers to seek blessings for their departed loved ones.

Ways to celebrate Mahalaya Amavasya include the recitation of hymns and chants, known as "Mahishasura Mardini Stotram," which recounts the slaying of the demon Mahishasura by Goddess Durga. Devotees also offer prayers and make offerings to their ancestors during this time, seeking their guidance and blessings.

Beyond the rituals, Mahalaya Amavasya imparts valuable lessons. It underscores the importance of gratitude and remembrance for our ancestors, recognizing the profound impact they have on our lives. It encourages us to acknowledge the foundations laid by those who came before us and to honour their legacy through our actions and deeds.

As we celebrate Mahalaya Amavasya within our school community, let us embrace the diversity it brings. The occasion transcends cultural and regional boundaries, symbolizing the universal values of gratitude, remembrance, and the interconnectedness of generations. It encourages us to appreciate and respect the traditions that contribute to the vibrant tapestry of our society.

In conclusion, Mahalaya Amavasya is not just a ritualistic observance; it is a day that connects us to our roots, our ancestors, and the divine feminine energy represented by Goddess Durga. As we immerse ourselves in the devotional fervour of this occasion, let us internalize the profound lessons it imparts and strive to carry forward the values of gratitude and remembrance in our lives.

Thank you, and may this Mahalaya Amavasya bring blessings, harmony, and a deep sense of connection to each one of you.

25

Navratri Begins

Respected faculty, dear students, and esteemed guests,

I stand before you today to illuminate the significance of the first day of Navratri, a vibrant festival that marks the beginning of a nine-night celebration dedicated to the divine feminine energy. As we explore the history, importance, ways to celebrate, and the lessons embedded in this auspicious occasion, let us embark on a journey that reflects the cultural and spiritual richness of Navratri.

The first day of Navratri signifies the commencement of a festival dedicated to honouring Goddess Durga, the embodiment of power, strength, and divine grace. The history of Navratri can be traced back to ancient Hindu scriptures, where the triumph of good over evil is celebrated through the narrative of Goddess Durga slaying the demon Mahishasura after nine nights of battle.

The importance of the first day lies in invoking the divine energy of Goddess Shaila Putri, the first form of Durga. Shaila Putri, meaning the daughter of the mountains, represents the pure and unblemished power of the goddess. Devotees offer prayers, perform rituals, and seek blessings for strength and courage as they embark on this nine-night spiritual journey.

Ways to celebrate the first day of Navratri are vibrant and diverse. Devotees adorn themselves in traditional attire, create elaborate displays of Kalash (sacred pot), and participate in the 'Ghatsthapana' ceremony, symbolizing the establishment of the divine energy in their homes. The lighting of lamps, recitation of hymns, and engaging in traditional dance forms such as Garba and Dandiya create an atmosphere of joy and devotion.

Beyond the festivities, the first day of Navratri imparts valuable lessons. Goddess Shaila Putri's embodiment as the daughter of the mountains teaches us the importance of unwavering strength and resilience in the face of challenges. As we invoke her energy, we are reminded to cultivate qualities of determination, courage, and fortitude in our personal and academic pursuits.

As we celebrate the first day of Navratri within our school community, let us embrace the diversity it brings. The occasion transcends cultural and regional boundaries, symbolizing universal values of strength, devotion, and the celebration of the divine feminine. It encourages us to appreciate and respect the traditions that contribute to the vibrant tapestry of our society.

In conclusion, the first day of Navratri is not just a festive beginning; it is a spiritual awakening that calls us to connect with the divine energy within and around us. As we immerse ourselves in the festivities, let us internalize the profound lessons it imparts and strive to embody the virtues of strength, resilience, and devotion in our lives.

Thank you, and may this first day of Navratri bring joy, blessings, and spiritual enlightenment to each one of you.

26

Navratri ends or Maha Navami

Respected faculty, dear students, and esteemed guests,

I stand before you today on the auspicious occasion of Maha Navami, the ninth and final day of the vibrant festival of Navratri. As we delve into the history, importance, ways to celebrate, and the lessons embedded in this culmination of the divine festivities, let us reflect on the spiritual significance that Maha Navami holds for each one of us.

Maha Navami marks the penultimate day of Navratri, a nine-night celebration dedicated to the worship of Goddess Durga and the triumph of good over evil. The history of Navratri and Maha Navami is deeply rooted in Hindu mythology, where the goddess is believed to have defeated the formidable demon Mahishasura after a fierce battle lasting nine nights.

The importance of Maha Navami lies in its symbolic representation of the victorious culmination of the divine feminine energy over the forces of darkness. It is a day when devotees intensify their prayers, seeking the blessings of Goddess Durga for strength, wisdom, and protection.

Ways to celebrate Maha Navami are diverse and spiritually enriching. Devotees participate in elaborate ceremonies, conduct special prayers, and engage in rituals that include the offering of flowers, fruits, and other sacred items to the goddess. Community events, including cultural performances and traditional dance forms, add to the festive atmosphere.

One of the significant customs on Maha Navami is the Ayudha Puja or Shastra Puja, where tools, instruments, and implements are worshipped. This tradition symbolizes the acknowledgment and gratitude for the tools that play a role in our daily lives and professions, emphasizing the sacredness of every aspect of our work and endeavours.

Beyond the rituals, Maha Navami imparts valuable lessons. The victorious conclusion of the Navratri festival reminds us of the power of perseverance, devotion, and righteousness in overcoming challenges. It teaches us that, with faith and dedication, we can conquer our inner demons and emerge stronger and wiser.

As we celebrate Maha Navami within our school community, let us embrace the diversity it brings. The occasion transcends cultural and regional boundaries, symbolizing universal values of triumph, devotion, and the celebration of the divine feminine. It encourages us to appreciate and respect the traditions that contribute to the vibrant tapestry of our society.

In conclusion, Maha Navami is not just a culmination of festivities; it is a spiritual crescendo that calls us to reflect on the triumph of good over evil and the indomitable spirit within each one of us. As we immerse ourselves in the celebrations, let us internalize the profound lessons it imparts and strive to embody the virtues of devotion, resilience, and victory in our lives.

Thank you, and may this Maha Navami bring joy, blessings, and spiritual fulfilment to each one of you.

27

Dusshera

Respected faculty, dear students, and honoured guests,

I stand before you today on the auspicious occasion of Dussehra, a festival that marks the victory of good over evil and carries profound lessons for each one of us. As we delve into the history, importance, ways to celebrate, and the lessons embedded in this symbolic day, let us embrace the spirit of triumph and righteousness that Dussehra embodies.

Dussehra, also known as Vijayadashami, is celebrated across India with great enthusiasm and devotion. The history of Dussehra finds its roots in the epic Ramayana, where Lord Rama, guided by the principles of righteousness, defeats the demon king Ravana after a fierce battle. This victory is commemorated on Dussehra, symbolizing the triumph of virtue over vice.

The importance of Dussehra extends beyond religious boundaries, offering universal lessons that resonate across cultures. It teaches us the significance of standing firm against injustice and upholding moral values even in the face of adversity. Dussehra serves as a reminder that, ultimately, truth and righteousness prevail over falsehood and wickedness.

Ways to celebrate Dussehra are diverse and culturally rich. In many regions, effigies of Ravana, Meghanada, and Kumbhakarna are burned to symbolize the destruction of evil forces. The day is marked by processions, cultural performances, and the exchange of good wishes among communities. It is also an occasion for families to come together, share festive meals, and engage in traditional rituals.

Beyond the festivities, Dussehra imparts valuable lessons. The story of Lord Rama's unwavering commitment to dharma (righteousness) encourages us to uphold moral principles in our own lives. It teaches us the importance of integrity, humility, and the strength that comes from staying true to one's values, even in the face of challenges.

As we celebrate Dussehra within our school community, let us embrace the diversity it brings. The occasion transcends cultural and regional boundaries, symbolizing universal values of courage, righteousness, and the victory of good over evil. It encourages us to appreciate and respect the traditions that contribute to the vibrant tapestry of our society.

In conclusion, Dussehra is not just a festival; it is a celebration of virtue, courage, and the indomitable spirit of righteousness. As we immerse ourselves in the festivities, let us internalize the profound lessons it imparts and strive to embody the virtues of truth, goodness, and moral integrity in our lives.

Thank you, and may this Dussehra bring joy, blessings, and the triumph of righteousness to each one of you.

28

Sharad Poornima

Respected faculty, dear students, and esteemed guests,

I stand before you today on the occasion of Sharad Purnima, a celebration that holds cultural and spiritual significance in our diverse tapestry. As we delve into the history, importance, ways to celebrate, and the lessons embedded in this auspicious day, let us explore the unique qualities that make Sharad Purnima a truly enchanting and meaningful observance.

Sharad Purnima, also known as Kojagiri Purnima, is celebrated on the full moon day of the Hindu lunar month of Ashwin, typically in October. This day carries special significance in various cultural and religious traditions, symbolizing the transition from the scorching heat of summer to the coolness of autumn.

The history of Sharad Purnima is intertwined with mythology, where it is believed that Lord Krishna performed the divine dance, known as the Raas Leela, with the Gopis on this night. The moonlit night of

Sharad Purnima is considered auspicious and is associated with tales of love, devotion, and spiritual awakening.

The importance of Sharad Purnima lies in its association with the harvest season, highlighting gratitude for the bounties of nature. It is believed that the moon's rays on this night contain special healing properties, and many observe the ritual of drinking cold milk left in the moonlight, symbolizing the absorption of positive energy.

Ways to celebrate Sharad Purnima are diverse and culturally rich. Devotees engage in night-long prayers, sing devotional songs, and participate in traditional dances, capturing the essence of joy and spiritual celebration. Many also keep fasts, perform charitable deeds, and decorate their homes to honour the divine energy associated with this auspicious night.

Beyond the festivities, Sharad Purnima imparts valuable lessons. The story of Lord Krishna's Raas Leela encourages us to seek spiritual joy and transcendental love. It teaches us the importance of harmony, devotion, and celebrating the beauty that surrounds us, both in nature and in our relationships with others.

As we celebrate Sharad Purnima within our school community, let us embrace the diversity it brings. The occasion transcends cultural and regional boundaries, symbolizing universal values of gratitude, devotion, and the celebration of the divine. It encourages us to appreciate and respect the traditions that contribute to the vibrant tapestry of our society.

In conclusion, Sharad Purnima is not just a celestial event; it is a celebration of spiritual awakening, gratitude, and the joyous transition from one season to another. As we immerse ourselves in the festivities, let us internalize the profound lessons it imparts and strive to embody the virtues of love, harmony, and appreciation in our lives.

Thank you, and may this Sharad Purnima bring joy, blessings, and a sense of spiritual fulfilment to each one of you.

29

Karva Chauth

Respected faculty, dear students, and esteemed guests,

I am honoured to address you today on the occasion of Karva Chauth, a festival that epitomizes love, commitment, and the enduring spirit of togetherness. As we explore the importance, history, ways to celebrate, and the lessons embedded in this beautiful tradition, let us delve into the cultural richness that Karva Chauth brings to our diverse community.

Karva Chauth, predominantly observed by married women, is a day of fasting that holds deep cultural and emotional significance. The roots of this tradition can be traced back to ancient Indian folklore, where tales of devotion and sacrifice form the foundation of the festival.

The history of Karva Chauth is often associated with the narrative of Queen Veervati. Legend has it that her unwavering dedication to her husband resulted in divine intervention, saving him from an untimely death. This tale symbolizes the profound bond between a husband and wife, and the lengths to which love and commitment can go.

The importance of Karva Chauth lies in its celebration of marital bliss and the enduring strength of the marital bond. On this day, married women observe a day-long fast, abstaining from food and water, praying for the well-being and longevity of their husbands. The fast is broken only after the sighting of the moon, a ritual that is often shared with the husband's active involvement.

Ways to celebrate Karva Chauth are steeped in tradition and ritual. Women dress in traditional attire, apply mehndi, and gather in groups to share stories, songs, and prayers. The evening sky is eagerly waited for the moonrise, which signals the end of the fast. This moment is often shared in a heartfelt ceremony, where husbands express their gratitude and love for their wives.

Beyond the rituals, Karva Chauth imparts valuable lessons. It emphasizes the significance of love, sacrifice, and commitment in marital relationships. The act of fasting is not merely a physical discipline but a symbol of the emotional and spiritual strength that binds couples together. It encourages us to cherish the deep connections we share with our life partners and appreciate the sacrifices made for the well-being of our loved ones.

As we celebrate Karva Chauth within our school community, let us embrace the diversity it brings. The occasion transcends cultural and regional boundaries, symbolizing universal values of love and dedication. It encourages us to appreciate and respect the traditions that contribute to the vibrant tapestry of our society.

In conclusion, Karva Chauth is more than a fast; it is a celebration of love, commitment, and the enduring strength of marital relationships. As we witness the festivities, let us internalize the profound lessons it imparts and strive to embody the virtues of devotion, sacrifice, and togetherness in our lives.

Thank you, and may this Karva Chauth bring joy, blessings, and strengthened bonds to each one of you.

30

Dhan Teras

Respected faculty, dear students, and honoured guests,

I am delighted to address you today on the auspicious occasion of Dhana Terash, a celebration that revolves around generosity, philanthropy, and the spirit of giving. As we explore the history, importance, ways to celebrate, and the lessons embedded in this unique tradition, let us delve into the cultural and social significance that Dhana Terash brings to our community.

Dhana Terash, also known as Dhanteras, marks the beginning of the five-day Diwali festival and holds a special place in our cultural and religious calendar. The word "Dhanteras" is derived from "Dhan," meaning wealth, and "Teras," signifying the thirteenth day of the lunar fortnight.

The history of Dhana Terash is rooted in Hindu mythology, where it is believed that on this day, Goddess Lakshmi emerged during the churning of the cosmic ocean. The tradition of purchasing and gifting precious metals such as gold and silver on Dhanteras is symbolic of inviting prosperity and good fortune into one's life.

The importance of Dhana Terash extends beyond the material realm. It is a day to express gratitude for the blessings of wealth and prosperity in our lives. Many families clean and decorate their homes, light lamps, and create rangolis to welcome Goddess Lakshmi, the divine bestower of wealth and abundance.

Ways to celebrate Dhana Terash are diverse and culturally rich. The purchase of new utensils, jewellery, or any form of precious metal is a common tradition, signifying the acquisition of wealth. Many also perform special prayers and rituals, seeking the blessings of Goddess Lakshmi for prosperity, happiness, and well-being.

Beyond the material celebrations, Dhana Terash imparts valuable lessons. It encourages us to adopt a generous and philanthropic mindset, recognizing that true wealth lies not just in possessions but in our ability to share and uplift those around us. The act of giving and contributing to the well-being of others fosters a sense of community and solidarity.

As we celebrate Dhana Terash within our school community, let us embrace the diversity it brings. The occasion transcends cultural and regional boundaries, symbolizing universal values of gratitude, generosity, and the celebration of wealth in its broader, inclusive sense. It encourages us to appreciate and respect the traditions that contribute to the vibrant tapestry of our society.

In conclusion, Dhana Terash is more than a day of material acquisitions; it is a celebration of gratitude, generosity, and the spiritual understanding that true wealth lies in the richness of our hearts. As we participate in the festivities, let us internalize the profound lessons it imparts and strive to embody the virtues of sharing, caring, and fostering prosperity for all.

Thank you, and may this Dhana Terash bring joy, blessings, and abundance to each one of you.

31

Diwali

Respected faculty, dear students, and esteemed guests,

I am honoured to stand before you on the joyous occasion of Diwali, a festival that illuminates our hearts and homes with the brilliance of lights, joy, and cultural richness. As we delve into the history, importance, ways to celebrate, and the lessons embedded in this festival of lights, let us collectively embrace the spirit of Diwali that resonates across our diverse school community.

Diwali, derived from the Sanskrit word "Deepavali," meaning a row of lights, is one of the most widely celebrated festivals in India and among Indian communities worldwide. Its roots lie in various mythological tales and cultural practices, symbolizing the triumph of light over darkness, knowledge over ignorance, and good over evil.

The history of Diwali finds resonance in different narratives, with one of the most significant being the return of Lord Rama, accompanied by Sita and

Lakshmana, from exile after defeating the demon king Ravana. The lighting of lamps by the people of Ayodhya to welcome and guide them home marks the essence of Diwali, portraying the victory of righteousness.

The importance of Diwali extends beyond religious boundaries, encapsulating the spirit of unity, joy, and renewed beginnings. It is a time when families come together, homes are adorned with lights and rangolis, and the air is filled with the fragrance of sweets and festive delicacies. The lighting of diyas (oil lamps), candles, and the bursting of fireworks create a vibrant and jubilant atmosphere.

Ways to celebrate Diwali are diverse and culturally rich. Families engage in cleaning and decorating their homes, symbolizing the removal of negativity and the welcoming of positive energy. The exchange of gifts, especially sweets and dry fruits, fosters a sense of generosity and camaraderie. Temples are adorned with lights, and prayers are offered to seek the blessings of the divine for prosperity and well-being.

Beyond the festivities, Diwali imparts valuable lessons. It reminds us of the significance of inner illumination, urging us to dispel the darkness of ignorance and prejudice within ourselves. The diversity of cultural practices during Diwali encourages us to appreciate and respect different traditions, fostering a sense of unity and understanding within our multicultural school community.

As we celebrate Diwali, let us embrace the diversity it brings. The occasion transcends cultural and regional boundaries, symbolizing universal values of joy, unity, and the victory of good over evil. It encourages us to appreciate and respect the traditions that contribute to the vibrant tapestry of our society.

In conclusion, Diwali is more than a festival of lights; it is a celebration of hope, positivity, and the enduring human spirit. As we immerse ourselves in the festivities, let us internalize the profound lessons it imparts and strive to embody the virtues of light, knowledge, and the triumph of goodness in our lives.

Thank you, and may this Diwali bring joy, blessings, and the radiance of light into each one of your lives.

32

Bhai Dooj

Respected faculty, dear students, and honoured guests,

I am privileged to address you on the occasion of Bhai Dooj, a festival that celebrates the beautiful bond between siblings. As we explore the history, importance, ways to celebrate, and the lessons embedded in this special day, let us cherish the unique and profound relationship between brothers and sisters that forms an integral part of our cultural fabric.

Bhai Dooj, also known as Bhai Phota or Bhai Tika, is a Hindu festival celebrated on the second day after Diwali. It holds immense significance in showcasing the love and camaraderie between siblings, symbolizing the unbreakable bond that transcends time and distance.

The history of Bhai Dooj is often linked to Hindu mythology, where it is believed that Lord Krishna visited his sister Subhadra after defeating the demon Narakasura. Subhadra lovingly welcomed her brother by applying tilak on his forehead and performing aarti, marking the tradition that is continued in the festival today.

The importance of Bhai Dooj lies in its celebration of the unique relationship between brothers and sisters. It is a day when sisters pray for the well-being, prosperity, and longevity of their brothers, applying the sacred tilak on their foreheads and performing aarti. Brothers, in turn, offer gifts and promise to protect and support their sisters throughout their lives.

Ways to celebrate Bhai Dooj are heartwarming and culturally rich. Families come together to share meals, exchange gifts, and participate in rituals that affirm the bond between siblings. Sisters prepare elaborate meals for their brothers, and the exchange of tokens of affection strengthens the familial ties. The occasion is not just about the physical presence but also about expressing love and care for siblings who may be far away.

Beyond the festivities, Bhai Dooj imparts valuable lessons. It underscores the significance of familial bonds and the unconditional support siblings provide to each other. The tradition of tilak and aarti emphasizes the sanctity of relationships, encouraging us to appreciate and respect the unique connections we share within our families.

As we celebrate Bhai Dooj within our school community, let us embrace the diversity it brings. The occasion transcends cultural and regional boundaries, symbolizing universal values of love, care, and the importance of family ties. It encourages us to appreciate and respect the traditions that contribute to the vibrant tapestry of our society.

In conclusion, Bhai Dooj is not just a festival; it is a celebration of siblinghood, love, and the enduring bond between brothers and sisters. As we participate in the festivities, let us internalize the profound lessons it imparts and strive to embody the virtues of love, support, and the strength that comes from these cherished relationships.

Thank you, and may this Bhai Dooj bring joy, blessings, and strengthened sibling bonds to each one of you.

Chhath Puja

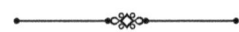

Respected faculty, dear students, and honoured guests,

I am honoured to address you today on the occasion of Chhath Puja, a festival deeply rooted in ancient traditions that holds immense cultural and spiritual significance. As we explore the history, importance, ways to celebrate, and the lessons embedded in this unique festival, let us delve into the rich tapestry of rituals and devotion that Chhath Puja brings to our diverse school community.

Chhath Puja, also known as Surya Shashti, is a Hindu festival dedicated to the worship of the Sun God, Surya, and Chhathi Maiya, the goddess who is believed to be the sister of Surya. Celebrated mainly in the states of Bihar, Jharkhand, and parts of Uttar Pradesh, Chhath Puja is a four-day festival culminating in the worship of the rising and setting sun.

The history of Chhath Puja is intricately connected to Hindu mythology, where it is believed that Draupadi and the Pandavas observed Chhath Puja to seek the blessings of the Sun God for prosperity and well-being. The festival is also associated with King Priyavrat, the son of the first Manu, who regained his kingdom and progeny through the observance of Chhath.

The importance of Chhath Puja lies in its reverence for the life-sustaining force of the Sun, symbolizing gratitude for energy and light. Devotees fast rigorously and offer prayers standing in water, with the rituals ranging from taking dips in rivers or ponds to preparing prasad (offerings) using traditional methods.

Ways to celebrate Chhath Puja are deeply rooted in tradition and ritual. Devotees wake up before sunrise, offer arghya (offerings) to the Sun God, and perform various rituals that include rigorous fasting and maintaining a strict code of conduct. The festival fosters a sense of community as families and neighbourhoods come together to participate in the rituals and celebrations.

Beyond the festivities, Chhath Puja imparts valuable lessons. It teaches us the importance of discipline, purity, and gratitude for the elements of nature that sustain life. The rituals performed during Chhath Puja are not just acts of devotion but also acts of environmental consciousness, emphasizing the need to protect and cherish our natural resources.

As we celebrate Chhath Puja within our school community, let us embrace the diversity it brings. The occasion transcends cultural and regional boundaries, symbolizing universal values of gratitude, discipline, and the celebration of nature. It encourages us to appreciate and respect the traditions that contribute to the vibrant tapestry of our society.

In conclusion, Chhath Puja is not just a festival; it is a spiritual journey that connects us to the elements of nature and reinforces our gratitude for life-sustaining forces. As we participate in the festivities, let us internalize the profound lessons it imparts and strive to embody the virtues of discipline, environmental consciousness, and gratitude in our lives.

Thank you, and may this Chhath Puja bring joy, blessings, and a deep sense of connection to each one of you.

34

Kartik Purnima

Respected faculty, dear students, and esteemed guests,

I am delighted to address you today on the occasion of Kartik Purnima, a festival that holds cultural, religious, and spiritual significance in various traditions. As we explore the history, importance, ways to celebrate, and the lessons embedded in this auspicious day, let us collectively immerse ourselves in the spiritual essence that Kartik Purnima brings to our diverse school community.

Kartik Purnima, also known as Deva-Deepawali or Tripuri Purnima, falls on the full moon day in the Hindu month of Kartik. This day holds profound importance in Hindu, Jain, and Sikh traditions, each celebrating it in their unique way.

The history of Kartik Purnima is interwoven with various mythological tales, including the victory of Lord Shiva over the demon Tripurasura, the descent of the Ganges River to Earth, and the attainment of Nirvana by

Lord Mahavira, the founder of Jainism. These stories signify the triumph of virtue over vice, the flow of spiritual knowledge, and the path to enlightenment.

The importance of Kartik Purnima transcends religious boundaries, symbolizing the pursuit of light, knowledge, and spiritual awakening. Devotees believe that performing acts of charity, taking holy dips in rivers, and lighting lamps on this day carry special significance, inviting blessings and dispelling darkness from one's life.

Ways to celebrate Kartik Purnima are diverse and spiritually enriching. Devotees wake up early, take a ritualistic bath, and offer prayers to deities. Lighting lamps and candles is a common practice, symbolizing the triumph of light over darkness. Many participate in religious processions and engage in acts of charity, fostering a sense of compassion and community.

Beyond the festivities, Kartik Purnima imparts valuable lessons. It encourages us to embrace the pursuit of knowledge and spiritual growth. The lighting of lamps signifies the illumination of one's inner self, dispelling ignorance and fostering wisdom. Acts of charity and kindness reinforce the importance of giving back to society and creating a positive impact on the lives of others.

As we celebrate Kartik Purnima within our school community, let us embrace the diversity it brings. The occasion transcends cultural and regional boundaries, symbolizing universal values of enlightenment, compassion, and the celebration of light. It encourages us to appreciate and respect the traditions that contribute to the vibrant tapestry of our society.

In conclusion, Kartik Purnima is not just a festival; it is a spiritual journey that calls us to illuminate our hearts and minds. As we participate in the festivities, let us internalize the profound lessons it imparts and strive to embody the virtues of knowledge, compassion, and the triumph of light in our lives.

Thank you, and may this Kartik Purnima bring joy, blessings, and spiritual enlightenment to each one of you.

35

Geeta Jayanti

Respected faculty, dear students, and esteemed guests,

I am honoured to address you today on the occasion of Geeta Jayanti, a day that holds profound significance in the realm of spirituality and philosophy. As we delve into the history, importance, ways to celebrate, and the lessons embedded in the teachings of the Bhagavad Gita, let us collectively embrace the wisdom that this sacred scripture imparts to our diverse school community.

Geeta Jayanti marks the anniversary of the day Lord Krishna imparted the teachings of the Bhagavad Gita to Arjuna on the battlefield of Kurukshetra. It falls on the Shukla Ekadashi of the Margashirsha month, emphasizing the timeless wisdom encapsulated in the verses of the Gita.

The Bhagavad Gita is a conversation between Lord Krishna and Arjuna, occurring in the midst of the Mahabharata war. It addresses the dilemmas faced by Arjuna and provides profound insights into the nature of life, duty, righteousness, and the path to spiritual realization. The Gita is revered as a philosophical guide, offering practical solutions to the challenges of existence.

The importance of Geeta Jayanti lies in the timeless relevance of the Bhagavad Gita's teachings. The scripture transcends religious boundaries, providing universal principles that guide individuals on the path of righteousness and self-realization. Geeta Jayanti serves as a reminder to reflect on these teachings and integrate them into our lives.

Ways to celebrate Geeta Jayanti are centred around studying and reciting verses from the Bhagavad Gita. Devotees participate in discourses, prayer meetings, and discussions on the profound insights offered by Lord Krishna. Many also engage in acts of charity and selfless service, aligning with the Gita's emphasis on performing one's duty without attachment to the fruits of actions.

Beyond the celebrations, Geeta Jayanti imparts valuable lessons. The teachings of the Bhagavad Gita encourage us to embrace our duties with a sense of detachment, focus on the present moment, and cultivate inner strength and resilience. The Gita serves as a guide for ethical decision-making, emphasizing the importance of righteousness and compassion in our actions.

As we celebrate Geeta Jayanti within our school community, let us embrace the diversity it brings. The occasion transcends cultural and regional boundaries, symbolizing universal values of wisdom, duty, and the pursuit of spiritual knowledge. It encourages us to appreciate and respect the philosophical traditions that contribute to the vibrant tapestry of our society.

In conclusion, Geeta Jayanti is not just a celebration of a historical event; it is an invitation to explore the profound teachings of the Bhagavad Gita and apply them in our daily lives. As we immerse ourselves in the festivities, let us internalize the timeless lessons it imparts and strive to embody the virtues of wisdom, righteousness, and spiritual realization.

Thank you, and may this Geeta Jayanti bring joy, blessings, and spiritual enlightenment to each one of you.

Dhanu Sankranti

Respected faculty, dear students, and honoured guests,

I am privileged to address you today on the occasion of Dhanu Sankranti, a festival that marks the transition of the Sun into the zodiac sign of Sagittarius, bringing with it cultural and spiritual significance. As we explore the history, importance, ways to celebrate, and the lessons embedded in this unique celebration, let us collectively embrace the essence of Dhanu Sankranti that enriches our diverse school community.

Dhanu Sankranti falls on the day when the Sun moves into the Sagittarius zodiac sign, marking the beginning of a new astronomical phase. The word "Dhanu" refers to Sagittarius, and "Sankranti" signifies the Sun's transition. This festival, although less widely known, carries deep cultural and agricultural connotations.

The importance of Dhanu Sankranti lies in its connection to the agricultural calendar and the changing seasons. It marks the beginning of the winter solstice, a period of shorter days and longer nights. In various regions of India, this festival is celebrated with a focus on expressing gratitude for the harvest, praying for agricultural prosperity, and invoking blessings for a bountiful season ahead.

Ways to celebrate Dhanu Sankranti vary across different communities. Many observe this day by taking a holy dip in sacred rivers, performing rituals, and offering prayers to the Sun God. Devotees' express gratitude for the agricultural abundance and seek blessings for the well-being of their crops. Traditional foods, especially those made from newly harvested crops, are prepared and shared as a symbol of communal harmony.

Beyond the festivities, Dhanu Sankranti imparts valuable lessons. It encourages us to appreciate the interconnectedness between nature, agriculture, and our lives. The rituals associated with the festival emphasize the importance of gratitude, humility, and recognizing the role of nature in sustaining our livelihoods.

As we celebrate Dhanu Sankranti within our school community, let us embrace the diversity it brings. The occasion transcends cultural and regional boundaries, symbolizing universal values of appreciation for nature, communal harmony, and gratitude. It encourages us to appreciate and respect the traditions that contribute to the vibrant tapestry of our society.

In conclusion, Dhanu Sankranti is not just an astronomical event; it is a celebration of the cyclical nature of life, agricultural abundance, and our connection to the environment. As we participate in the festivities, let us internalize the profound lessons it imparts and strive to embody the virtues of gratitude, humility, and environmental consciousness in our lives.

Thank you, and may this Dhanu Sankranti bring joy, blessings, and prosperity to each one of you.

37

Republic Day

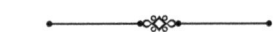

Respected faculty, dear students, and honoured guests,

I am delighted to address you today on the occasion of Republic Day, a momentous day in the history of our great nation. As we come together to commemorate the adoption of the Constitution of India, let us reflect on the importance, history, ways to celebrate, and the enduring lessons that Republic Day imparts to our diverse school community.

Republic Day, celebrated annually on January 26th, marks the day when the Constitution of India came into effect in 1950, replacing the Government of India Act (1935). This transition to a sovereign, socialist, secular, and democratic republic laid the foundation for the democratic principles that guide our nation today.

The importance of Republic Day lies in its commemoration of the values enshrined in the Constitution - justice, liberty, equality, and fraternity. It signifies the day when India transitioned to a republic with a government chosen by its citizens. Republic Day serves as a reminder of the sacrifices made by our forefathers and the responsibility each of us carries to uphold the democratic ideals that form the bedrock of our nation.

Ways to celebrate Republic Day are both solemn and joyous. The day begins with the grandeur of the Republic Day Parade in the capital, showcasing the military might, cultural diversity, and technological prowess of our nation. Schools and communities across the country organize flag hoisting ceremonies, patriotic songs, and cultural programs to honour the spirit of the day.

The celebration of Republic Day is not merely a display of national pride; it is an affirmation of our commitment to the principles of justice, liberty, equality, and fraternity. The unfurling of the national flag and the singing of the national anthem evoke a sense of unity and pride among citizens. It is a day when we collectively reaffirm our allegiance to the democratic values that guide our nation.

Beyond the festivities, Republic Day imparts valuable lessons. It reminds us that the strength of a nation lies in the active participation of its citizens. The democratic ideals of the Constitution call upon each of us to contribute to the betterment of society, to strive for justice, and to uphold the principles of equality and fraternity.

As we celebrate Republic Day within our school community, let us embrace the diversity it brings. The occasion transcends cultural and regional boundaries, symbolizing universal values of democracy, unity, and patriotism. It encourages us to appreciate and respect the democratic traditions that contribute to the vibrant tapestry of our society.

In conclusion, Republic Day is not just a commemoration; it is a celebration of the democratic spirit that unites us as Indians. As we participate in the festivities, let us internalize the profound lessons it imparts and strive to embody the virtues of justice, liberty, equality, and fraternity in our lives.

Thank you, and may this Republic Day bring joy, blessings, and a renewed commitment to the democratic ideals that define our great nation. Jai Hind!

ns

Independence Day of India

Good [morning/afternoon/evening], and a warm welcome to each one of you as we gather to commemorate a significant moment in our nation's history - the Independence Day of India. Today, we come together not only to celebrate the freedom we cherish but also to reflect on the importance of history and the lessons it imparts to us.

As we stand on the shoulders of those who fought for our independence, it is crucial that we understand the sacrifices made and the struggles faced. History serves as a powerful teacher, offering us valuable insights into the past, shaping our present, and guiding us towards a more enlightened future.

In the grand tapestry of our nation's journey, every thread is essential. From the sacrifices of our freedom fighters to the tireless efforts of individuals who shaped the destiny of our country, their stories are a testament to resilience, unity, and unwavering determination.

As we celebrate Independence Day, let us not merely revel in the festivities but also take a moment to appreciate the historical significance of this day. It's an opportunity to instil in ourselves and our students a sense of pride in our heritage, fostering a deep connection with our roots.

To make this occasion memorable, let's explore ways in which we can infuse history into the celebrations. Consider organizing informative sessions or exhibitions that showcase pivotal moments in our struggle for independence. Invite speakers who can share their insights, providing a personal touch to the narratives that textbooks might not capture.

Additionally, let's encourage students to express their understanding of history through creative outlets. Art exhibitions, essay competitions, or even theatrical performances can be powerful mediums to convey the richness of our past and the importance of preserving our cultural identity.

Moreover, instilling a sense of responsibility towards our nation is paramount. As Mahatma Gandhi once said, "You must be the change you want to see in the world." Let's inspire our students to embody these words, fostering a spirit of active citizenship and social responsibility.

In conclusion, as we celebrate Independence Day, let us not only revel in the joyous festivities but also appreciate the profound lessons history imparts. By understanding our past, we equip ourselves and the generations to come with the knowledge and values necessary to build a harmonious and progressive future.

Thank you, and may we continue to cherish and uphold the spirit of independence. Jai Hind!

Gandhi Jayanti

Ladies and gentlemen, esteemed faculty, and dear students,

Today, we gather to commemorate a man whose life has left an indelible mark on the pages of history - Mahatma Gandhi. As we celebrate Gandhi Jayanti, it is crucial to reflect on the profound impact this visionary leader had on our nation and the world.

Born on October 2, 1869, in Porbandar, Gujarat, Gandhi emerged as the epitome of non-violent resistance against oppression. His philosophy of truth and non-violence, or 'Satyagraha,' became the guiding light for our nation's struggle for independence from British rule.

Gandhi's teachings extend beyond his role in India's freedom struggle. His principles of tolerance, unity, and the pursuit of truth are timeless and resonate with us even today. Gandhi Jayanti is not just a day to remember a historical figure, but an opportunity to internalize the values he stood for.

On this day, let us engage in activities that promote peace, harmony, and social responsibility. Consider organizing discussions on Gandhian philosophy, participating in community service projects, or even practicing a day of silence to cultivate inner reflection.

Gandhi's life offers numerous lessons for us all. His ability to lead through compassion, perseverance, and moral conviction should inspire us to be better individuals. Let us learn from his commitment to social justice, simplicity, and the pursuit of a life aligned with one's principles.

In conclusion, as we commemorate Gandhi Jayanti, let us not merely observe but internalize the essence of his teachings. Our actions, both individually and collectively, can contribute to the creation of a more just and compassionate society. Through our commitment to truth and non-violence, we can strive to make the world a better place.

Thank you, and let us carry forward the legacy of Mahatma Gandhi in our hearts and actions.

40

Children's Day of India

Ladies and gentlemen, esteemed faculty, cherished students, and honoured guests,

I stand before you on this special occasion of Children's Day, a day that celebrates the essence of childhood and the significance it holds in our lives. As we gather here today, let us take a moment to reflect on the history, importance, ways to celebrate, and the valuable lessons embedded in this joyful day.

Children's Day traces its roots back to the visionary leader, Jawaharlal Nehru, whose love for children inspired the declaration of his birthday, November 14th, as Children's Day in India. This day not only honours his legacy but also serves as a universal celebration of the innocence, potential, and happiness that children bring to the world.

The importance of Children's Day lies in recognizing the rights of every child to a happy and fulfilling childhood. It serves as a reminder for us, as a society and educational institution, to prioritize the well-being and holistic development of our young minds. Today, we reaffirm our commitment to fostering an environment that nurtures creativity, curiosity, and resilience.

Now, let's explore the various ways we can celebrate Children's Day. Beyond the traditional distribution of sweets and cultural programs, let's engage in activities that encourage collaboration, imagination, and play. Whether it's organizing fun games, storytelling sessions, or even involving our students in decision-making processes, let's make this day truly memorable for them.

However, celebrations aside, Children's Day is also an opportunity to impart valuable lessons. As educators, we play a crucial role in shaping the minds of the next generation. Let's use this occasion to instil the importance of empathy, kindness, and responsibility in our students. By fostering a sense of social awareness and moral values, we contribute to the development of responsible citizens who will positively impact the world.

On this day, let's not forget the core values that guide us as a community. We must strive to create a safe, inclusive, and nurturing environment where every child feels heard, valued, and supported in their unique journey of growth and learning.

In conclusion, Children's Day is not just a day of celebration; it is a reminder of our collective responsibility to shape a brighter future. As we commemorate this day, let us recommit ourselves to the well-being and education of our children, for they are the architects of tomorrow.

Thank you for your attention, and may this Children's Day be filled with joy, laughter, and meaningful reflections for each and every one of us.

41

Teacher's Day in India

Ladies and gentlemen, esteemed faculty, and dear students,

I stand before you today with immense joy and pride as we come together to celebrate Teacher's Day, a day dedicated to honouring the pillars of knowledge and guidance in our lives. As we embark on this special occasion, let us take a moment to delve into the history, understand the significance, explore ways to celebrate, and reflect on the invaluable lessons that teachers impart.

Teacher's Day in India is celebrated on the birth anniversary of Dr. Sarvepalli Radhakrishnan, a renowned philosopher, scholar, and India's second President. Dr. Radhakrishnan's commitment to education made him an iconic figure, and it is in his honour that we pay tribute to all educators on this day. His belief in the transformative power of education underscores the importance of teachers in shaping the future of our nation.

Teachers play a pivotal role in sculpting young minds, fostering a love for learning, and nurturing the leaders of tomorrow. Today, we express our gratitude to our dedicated educators for their unwavering commitment to shaping the intellect and character of our students.

Now, let's talk about ways to celebrate Teacher's Day. It goes beyond the customary rituals of flowers and gifts; it's about acknowledging and appreciating the hard work, dedication, and passion that teachers bring to the classroom. Consider organizing student performances, heartfelt messages, or even a small event to honour and recognize their efforts.

As we celebrate, let us not forget the profound lessons our teachers instil in us. Lessons that extend beyond textbooks - the importance of resilience, empathy, and the pursuit of knowledge. It is through these lessons that our teachers become not just instructors but mentors, guiding us through the journey of self-discovery.

In conclusion, Teacher's Day is a moment for us to express our gratitude, celebrate the commitment to education, and reflect on the timeless lessons imparted by our teachers. As we honour their contributions today, let us commit to carrying the torch of knowledge forward, appreciating the impact teachers have on our lives.

Thank you for your attention, and Happy Teacher's Day to all the educators who shape the destiny of our students and contribute to the progress of our society.

42

Honesty

Good morning! Today, I want to talk to you about a fundamental value that is the cornerstone of integrity and trust - honesty.

In a world filled with complexities, where we face various challenges, honesty remains a timeless virtue that guides us towards righteousness and moral strength. As members of this school community, it is our shared responsibility to uphold and cherish the value of honesty.

Allow me to share a short parable with you. Once upon a time, in a small village, there lived a young boy named Ankit. Ankit was known for his honesty, a trait he inherited from his wise grandmother. One day, while playing in the village square, he found a wallet with a considerable sum of money. Instead of keeping it for himself, Ankit chose the path of honesty and returned the wallet to its rightful owner. The grateful owner, impressed by Ankit's integrity, not only thanked him but also became a lifelong friend and mentor. Ankit's honesty not only enriched his own life but also had a positive ripple effect on the entire village.

Similarly, in our school community, honesty is not just about avoiding lies or deceit. It's about being true to ourselves, to each other, and to the principles that define us. When we choose honesty, we contribute to an environment of trust and mutual respect, fostering a community where individuals can thrive and achieve their full potential.

As students, you are the future leaders, scientists, artists, and thinkers of our society. Honesty is a compass that will guide you through the complexities of life, helping you navigate challenges with integrity. Remember that your actions not only reflect on yourselves but also on the values we collectively uphold as a school.

To our dedicated staff, your commitment to honesty serves as a guiding light for our students. Your integrity sets the standard for the learning environment we strive to create, emphasizing the importance of ethical conduct in both education and life.

In conclusion, let us embrace honesty as a guiding principle in our daily lives. As we navigate the journey of education together, let honesty be the compass that points us in the direction of moral courage and ethical conduct. It is through our commitment to honesty that we build a community of trust, respect, and shared values.

Thank you for your attention, and let us continue to foster a culture of honesty within the walls of our beloved school.

43

Compassion

Good [morning/afternoon/evening], and thank you for gathering today. Today, I'd like to talk about a virtue that I believe is the heartbeat of any thriving community – compassion.

Compassion is not just a word; it's a force that binds us together, creating a nurturing environment where empathy and understanding flourish. As we navigate the challenges of school life, it becomes paramount that we embrace this quality wholeheartedly.

Allow me to share a little parable with you. Once upon a time, in a school much like ours, there were two students - let's call them Alex and Taylor. Alex was known for academic brilliance, while Taylor struggled with subjects that required a bit more effort. One day, Alex noticed Taylor tirelessly working on a challenging assignment. Instead of gloating over their own accomplishments, Alex decided to offer a helping hand.

Now, the interesting part is that the subject Taylor needed assistance with happened to be Alex's strong suit. With patience and understanding, Alex not only helped

Taylor grasp the concept but also ignited a friendship built on compassion and support.

This parable illustrates how compassion can transform our school into a community where every student and staff member feel seen, valued, and supported.

Compassion goes beyond sympathy; it's about taking that extra step to understand and alleviate someone else's struggles. As the principal, I urge each one of you to cultivate this virtue in your daily interactions.

For students, it means reaching out to your classmates, offering a helping hand when someone is struggling, and recognizing that success is sweeter when shared. Remember, your academic achievements are not just individual triumphs but collective victories.

To our dedicated staff members, I encourage you to be compassionate mentors. Each student is a unique individual with different strengths and challenges. By fostering an atmosphere of understanding, you not only contribute to their academic growth but also shape them into compassionate individuals ready to face the world beyond these school walls.

In conclusion, let's make compassion a cornerstone of our school community. The ability to empathize, support, and uplift one another is what sets us apart. As we continue our journey together, let compassion guide our actions and strengthen the bonds that make our school a truly exceptional place.

Thank you, and let's continue to foster a culture of compassion within our school.

44

Generosity

Ladies and gentlemen, esteemed faculty, and our wonderful students,

Good morning! Today, I want to share a few thoughts on a virtue that can truly transform our school community – generosity.

Generosity is like sunshine; it brightens not only the recipient's day but also warms the heart of the giver. In our school, we are fortunate to have a culture of kindness, and today, I want to encourage each and every one of you to embrace the spirit of generosity.

Now, let me share a little parable to illustrate the power of generosity. Once upon a time, in a small village, there was a kind old woman known for her generosity. She had a magical pot that could produce unlimited soup. One day, a hungry traveller asked her for some food. Without hesitation, she filled his bowl with her magical soup. To her surprise, the more she gave, the more the pot produced.

The traveller, overwhelmed by her generosity, asked, "Why are you so kind?" She replied, "Because kindness, my friend, is a never-ending resource." The traveller, inspired by her words, carried the spirit of generosity forward, and the village flourished.

Just like that magical pot, our capacity for generosity is boundless. Whether it's lending a helping hand to a struggling classmate or sharing knowledge with a colleague, each act of generosity contributes to the growth and strength of our school community.

Students, imagine the impact we could make if we embraced generosity in our daily interactions. Helping a friend with homework, welcoming new students with open arms, or simply offering a kind word - these small acts create ripples of positivity that reverberate throughout our school.

Staff, your dedication and hard work are the backbone of our school. By fostering a culture of generosity, we can enhance the collaborative spirit that makes our institution thrive. Share your expertise, support your colleagues, and together, we can create an environment where everyone feels valued.

In closing, I challenge each of you to be like that magical pot, overflowing with generosity. Let us be the catalysts for positive change within our school community. As we extend a hand of kindness, remember that the true magic lies in the connections we forge and the bonds we strengthen.

Thank you for your attention, and let's make our school a place where generosity becomes a guiding principle for all.

45

Respect

Ladies and gentlemen, esteemed faculty, and our wonderful students,

Good morning to each and every one of you. Today, I'd like to address a topic that lies at the core of a thriving school community – respect. It's not just a word; it's a fundamental value that shapes our interactions, fosters a positive environment, and ultimately contributes to the success of our school.

Now, let me share a humorous parable to highlight the importance of respect. Imagine a forest where different animals coexist - the wise owl, the fast cheetah, the diligent ant, and the playful monkey. One day, they decided to organize a grand talent show. The owl, with its wisdom, suggested they should all appreciate each other's unique talents and not judge based on their differences.

During the talent show, the ant showcased its strength in lifting objects many times its size, the cheetah demonstrated its incredible speed, and the monkey entertained everyone with its acrobatics. However, as the owl was about to present its talent - a thoughtful and insightful speech - the other animals burst into laughter, questioning how wisdom could be a talent.

The owl, undeterred, calmly explained that each talent is valuable in its own way, just like every person in our school community possesses unique qualities. It's the diversity of talents and perspectives that makes our school vibrant and dynamic. By respecting and appreciating these differences, we create an environment where everyone can thrive.

Now, let's apply this parable to our daily lives here at school. Respect starts with acknowledging and appreciating the diverse talents and qualities each of us brings to the table. Whether it's in the classroom, on the sports field, or during extracurricular activities, let's celebrate the uniqueness in each other.

Respecting one another also means listening actively and valuing different opinions. Our school is a microcosm of the world, and learning how to respectfully disagree fosters growth and understanding. As we navigate the challenges of academics and social interactions, remember that respect is the compass guiding us.

I encourage each of you to take a moment to reflect on your actions and words. Are they contributing positively to our school's culture of respect? Let's strive to be mindful of how we treat our peers, teachers, and staff members.

In conclusion, my dear students and faculty, respect is the foundation upon which our school community stands. Embrace the diversity of talents, perspectives, and backgrounds that make us unique. By doing so, we not only enrich our own lives but also contribute to the collective success of our school.

Thank you for your attention, and let's continue to build a school where respect is not just a value but a way of life.

46

Responsibility

Ladies and gentlemen, esteemed faculty, and our incredible students,

Good morning! Today, I'd like to talk to you about a topic that is fundamental to our success as individuals and as a community - Responsibility.

Responsibility is not just a word; it's a commitment we make to ourselves and those around us. It's the cornerstone of a thriving society. As students and educators, each of us plays a vital role in shaping the future, and that begins with being responsible.

Let me share a little parable with you to drive this point home. Once upon a time, in a land not too different from ours, there was a wise old turtle named Tessa. Tessa lived in a bustling forest alongside various animals, each with their own responsibilities.

One day, the animals noticed that the river near their home was getting polluted. Instead of blaming each other or waiting for someone else to take action, they decided to come together and clean up the mess. Tessa, being the wise turtle, took charge and organized the effort.

The animals worked diligently, each playing their part. The birds flew to gather trash, the beavers constructed recycling bins, and the rabbits organized cleanup schedules. Even the mischievous monkeys lent a helping hand by creating catchy slogans to raise awareness.

Through their collective responsibility, the once-polluted river became a symbol of environmental stewardship. The animals learned that taking responsibility not only improved their immediate surroundings but also created a better environment for future generations.

Now, let's bring this parable closer to home. In our school community, we all have responsibilities. Students, your responsibility is not just to excel academically but to contribute positively to the school culture. Attend classes, complete your assignments, and show kindness to your fellow students.

Teachers and staff, your responsibility is not only to impart knowledge but to inspire and guide our students towards becoming responsible individuals. Create an environment where curiosity flourishes, and respect for one another is paramount.

Responsibility, much like the pieces of a puzzle, fits together to create a harmonious picture. It's about accountability, integrity, and doing what needs to be done even when no one is watching.

As the saying goes, "With great power comes great responsibility." We all have the power to influence our community positively, and with that power comes the responsibility to act ethically and with care.

Let's continue building our school as a haven of responsibility. Whether it's picking up after ourselves in the cafeteria or supporting a classmate in need, these seemingly small actions contribute to the vibrant tapestry of our school community.

In conclusion, let us embrace responsibility with open arms. Like Tessa and her friends in the parable, we can create positive change when we all take ownership of our actions. Together, we will not only thrive academically but also nurture a culture of responsibility that will extend far beyond the walls of our school.

Thank you for your attention, and let's make this year a testament to the power of responsibility!

47

Be True to Yourself

Good morning! Today, I want to talk about a simple yet profound concept that has the power to shape our lives in extraordinary ways: being true to yourself.

In this journey called life, it's easy to get caught up in the expectations and opinions of others. We often find ourselves trying to fit into moulds that society or our peers have created for us. However, I want to emphasize the importance of staying true to who you are, embracing your uniqueness, and letting your authenticity shine.

Now, let me share a humorous parable to illustrate this point:

Once upon a time in a forest, there were three trees – an oak, a pine, and a willow. They were all beautiful in their own way, but they envied each other's strengths. The oak wished it could sway in the breeze like the willow, the willow longed for the height of the oak, and the pine wished for the strong branches of the oak.

One day, a wise old owl visited the forest and noticed their discontent. The owl said, "Dear trees, each of you has unique qualities that make you special. Embrace your own strengths, for that is what makes the forest diverse and beautiful."

The trees took the owl's advice to heart and started appreciating their individual characteristics. The oak stood tall, providing shade and shelter. The willow gracefully danced in the breeze, bringing joy to all who saw. The pine stood strong, its branches supporting various creatures.

Just like those trees, each of you possesses unique talents and qualities. Embrace them. Don't be afraid to be different, for it is our differences that make our school community vibrant and rich.

Being true to yourself requires self-awareness and courage. It means listening to your inner voice, following your passions, and staying authentic even when faced with challenges. It's about recognizing that it's okay to be imperfect because perfection is not the goal - genuine self-expression is.

Remember, the path to success and happiness is not about conforming to someone else's idea of who you should be. It's about discovering and embracing your true self.

In conclusion, let us celebrate our diversity and individuality. Embrace your strengths, acknowledge your weaknesses, and continue to grow into the amazing individuals you are destined to become. Be true to yourself, and you'll not only find success but also genuine fulfilment.

Thank you for your attention, and let's make this school year a journey of self-discovery and authenticity.

48

Cooperation

Ladies and gentlemen, esteemed faculty, and dear students,

Good morning! Today, I want to talk about a fundamental principle that can make our school not just a place of learning but a community that thrives - cooperation.

Imagine a group of ants working together to build a magnificent anthill. Each ant contributes its unique skills, and together, they create something far greater than what any one ant could achieve alone. In our school, each one of you is like an ant, and through cooperation, we can build something extraordinary.

Cooperation isn't just about working together; it's about understanding and appreciating each other's strengths and weaknesses. It's about recognizing that, like puzzle pieces, we fit together to create a complete picture. As students, your success is not just an individual triumph but a collective achievement that elevates the entire school.

Now, let me share a humorous parable to illustrate the power of cooperation:

Once upon a time in the animal kingdom, the lion, the king of the jungle, decided to organize a talent show. He invited all the animals to showcase their unique skills. The birds sang melodiously, the monkeys performed acrobatics, and the turtles told slow but witty jokes. However, there was one animal missing - the snail.

Curious, the lion asked the snail why it didn't participate. The snail replied, "Well, I have a special talent, but it takes a bit of time." Intrigued, the lion insisted that the snail perform.

So, the snail started its act, and the entire audience waited patiently. After what seemed like an eternity, the snail finally reached the centre of the stage and exclaimed, "Ta-da!" It had drawn a beautiful, intricate masterpiece.

The lesson here is that even if it takes time for some to contribute, their unique talents can make a significant impact. Patience and cooperation allow everyone's strengths to shine.

As a school, let's embrace the diversity of talents, backgrounds, and perspectives within our community. When we cooperate, we create an environment where everyone feels valued and supported, leading to a more enriching educational experience.

Teachers, you play a crucial role as guides in fostering cooperation. Encourage group projects, where students can learn to collaborate and leverage each other's strengths. Students, be open to working with different peers - you might discover hidden talents and develop lasting friendships.

In conclusion, cooperation isn't just a concept; it's a mindset that can transform our school into a thriving community. Let's work together, learn together, and grow together. Remember, just like those ants building a magnificent anthill, we are capable of achieving greatness when we cooperate.

Thank you, and let's make cooperation a cornerstone of our school's success!

49

Courage

Ladies and gentlemen, esteemed faculty, and my wonderful students,

Good morning! Today, I stand before you to talk about a quality that defines greatness in individuals - courage.

Courage is not just about - facing life-threatening situations, but also about confronting our fears, standing up for what is right, and embracing challenges with an unwavering spirit. I want to share a parable that illustrates this point.

Once upon a time, in a small village, there was a quirky chicken named Cluckington. Now, Cluckington was known for being the most adventurous chicken in the coop. One day, he decided - he wanted to explore the other side of the farmyard fence. The other chickens were skeptical, warning him about the dangers that awaited.

But Cluckington, with a twinkle in his eye, hopped over the fence and found himself in a vast, unknown world. As he strutted along, he encountered various animals and faced numerous challenges. Despite his fears, he pressed on, gaining new experiences and making unlikely friends.

In the end, Cluckington returned to the coop, not only with tales of his adventures but also with newfound wisdom. The other chickens, inspired by his courage, began to look beyond the safety of the coop and explore the possibilities that lay outside.

Just like Cluckington, each of you has the potential for courage within. It might be the courage to speak up in class, to stand against injustice, or to pursue your dreams despite doubts. Embrace those moments, for it is through courage that we grow and make a lasting impact.

Now, let's add a sprinkle of humour to this discussion of courage. Have you ever noticed how sometimes our fears are like little monsters under our beds? They seem enormous in the darkness, but when we turn on the light and face them, we realize they were just shadows all along.

So, my dear students and staff, let's turn on the light and face our fears together. Whether it's tackling a difficult subject, approaching someone new, or trying something outside of your comfort zone, remember that courage is not the absence of fear, but the triumph over it.

In the face of challenges, let's be like Cluckington, the adventurous chicken, and take that leap of faith. The journey might be filled with uncertainties, but it is through courage that we discover our true potential and leave an indelible mark on the world.

Thank you, and may your days be filled with the courage to chase your dreams!

50

Student's Empowerment

Ladies and gentlemen, esteemed faculty, dedicated staff, and most importantly, our bright and talented students,

Today, I stand before you to address a topic that is crucial in shaping not just the future of our students but the trajectory of our society as a whole-student empowerment in the modern-day scenario.

In an era defined by rapid technological advancements and ever-evolving global challenges, the empowerment of our students has never been more critical. As we navigate the complexities of the 21st century, it is imperative that we equip our students not only with academic knowledge but also with the skills, resilience, and mindset necessary to thrive in an ever-changing world.

Empowering students means fostering a sense of agency and self-confidence, enabling them to take control of their own learning journey. Our educational institution is not just a place to acquire facts; it is a platform for personal growth, self-discovery, and the development of critical thinking skills. It is here that students learn not only about the subjects in their curriculum but also about themselves-about their passions, strengths, and the unique contributions they can make to society.

As educators and mentors, it is our responsibility to create an environment that encourages curiosity and creativity. We must cultivate a culture that values diversity of thought and encourages students to explore their interests beyond the confines of textbooks. Let's embrace a teaching philosophy that promotes collaboration, problem-solving, and adaptability—the very skills that will empower our students to navigate the challenges of the modern world.

Moreover, student empowerment extends beyond the classroom. It involves instilling a sense of social responsibility and global awareness. Our students are not just the leaders of tomorrow; they are the catalysts for positive change today. By fostering empathy and a commitment to social justice, we empower our students to be active and compassionate members of society.

I urge the faculty and staff to continue providing mentorship and guidance, recognizing the unique potential in each student. Let's create spaces for open dialogue and ensure that the voices of our students are not just heard but valued. By doing so, we not only empower individuals but contribute to the collective strength of our educational community.

In conclusion, let us commit to a holistic approach to education-one that goes beyond test scores and embraces the holistic development of our students. As we empower them with knowledge, skills, and a sense of purpose, we are laying the foundation for a generation that will lead with innovation, resilience, and a deep understanding of the world.

Thank you for your dedication to the empowerment of our students, and let us continue working together to shape a brighter and more empowered future.

51

Gratitude

Ladies and gentlemen, esteemed faculty, and our bright students, good morning. Today, I want to share a few thoughts on a theme that has the power to transform our lives - gratitude.

In the fast-paced world we live in, it's easy to get caught up in the hustle and forget to pause and appreciate the moments that shape us. Let me begin with a little parable to illustrate the essence of gratitude.

Once upon a time, in a bustling town, there lived a man who possessed a magical mirror. This mirror had the power to reflect the true essence of a person's heart. One day, a skeptical traveller approached the man and asked to see his reflection. To his surprise, the mirror revealed not his image, but scenes of people helping him throughout his life - his parents, teachers, friends, and even strangers. The traveller, moved by this revelation, understood the importance of gratitude, realizing that behind every success and joy, there were countless acts of kindness.

My dear students and staff, we too have our mirrors. In the journey of education, we encounter countless individuals who contribute to our growth and success. Our teachers, who tirelessly nurture our minds; our colleagues, who make the workplace a second home; and our friends, who stand by us through thick and thin. Today, let's take a moment to reflect upon our mirrors and express gratitude.

It's not just about saying 'thank you'; it's about understanding the depth of gratitude. As the saying goes, "Gratitude turns what we have into enough." It's a powerful force that can transform our attitudes, relationships, and ultimately our entire school community.

Let me share a humorous anecdote to lighten the mood. There was a teacher who received a beautifully wrapped gift from a student. Excitedly, she unwrapped it to find an apple. Puzzled, she asked the student, "Why an apple?" The student replied, "Because my mom says you're the core of our education!"

Now, while we may not always receive literal apples, the sentiment behind the gesture holds true. Teachers, staff, and students - we're all essential parts of this educational ecosystem. It's essential to acknowledge and appreciate each other for the vital roles we play.

In the spirit of gratitude, I encourage you to take a moment each day to express thanks. Whether it's a kind word, a gesture of appreciation, or a simple acknowledgment, these small acts can create a ripple effect of positivity.

As we navigate the challenges of academia, let's not forget the power of a grateful heart. In the words of Oprah Winfrey, "Be thankful for what you have; you'll end up having more. If you concentrate on what you don't have, you will never, ever have enough."

In conclusion, let gratitude be the guiding light in our journey of learning and growth. Let's cherish the relationships, appreciate the efforts, and acknowledge the collective strength that makes our school a beacon of knowledge and warmth.

Thank you for your attention, and let's make gratitude a way of life in our school community.

52

Perseverance

Ladies and gentlemen, esteemed faculty, and our resilient students,

I stand before you today to discuss a virtue that is not only relevant to our academic journey but resonates deeply with life itself - perseverance. In the face of challenges and obstacles, it is the unwavering commitment to our goals that defines our character and ensures success.

Now, let me share a humorous parable to illustrate the essence of perseverance. Imagine a determined snail named Sam who set out on a journey to reach the top of a towering sunflower. Despite the odds, Sam persistently climbed, never deterred by the slow pace or the enormous task at hand.

In our own pursuits, we encounter hurdles that might seem insurmountable. Just like Sam, we must cultivate the spirit of perseverance, understanding that progress is often gradual, but the journey is what shapes us.

As students, you face academic challenges that may appear daunting. Remember, success is not always about the speed of your climb but the tenacity to keep moving forward. A setback is not a roadblock; it's a detour that may lead you to unexpected opportunities.

To our dedicated staff, your perseverance is the driving force behind our students' success. Your commitment to their growth and education inspires them to navigate their academic sunflowers with courage and determination.

Let's embrace challenges as opportunities for growth. In the words of Winston Churchill, "Success is not final, failure is not fatal: It is the courage to continue that counts."

As we navigate this journey together, let's celebrate not only the destination but the lessons learned along the way. Perseverance is not just about reaching the top; it's about evolving into resilient individuals capable of conquering any challenge.

In conclusion, let's foster a culture of perseverance within our school community. Let the story of Sam, the determined snail, serve as a reminder that slow and steady progress, coupled with unwavering determination, leads to the sweet taste of success.

Thank you for your attention, and may our collective perseverance light the path for a brighter future.

53

Family

Ladies and gentlemen, esteemed faculty, and our wonderful students,

Good morning to each one of you. Today, I stand before you to discuss a topic that is close to our hearts and plays a crucial role in shaping our lives - family.

Our school is more than just a place of learning; it's a community where we build connections that go beyond textbooks and classrooms. Just like our school family, our biological families form the foundation of who we are. They provide the support, love, and guidance that shapes our character and values.

In the hustle and bustle of our daily lives, it's easy to overlook the significance of family. Whether it's the warmth of a parent's hug, the laughter shared with siblings, or the wisdom passed down through generations, these moments contribute to the rich tapestry of our lives.

Students, as you navigate through your academic journey, remember that your family is your anchor. They celebrate your victories and stand by you during challenges. Take a moment to express gratitude for the sacrifices they make to ensure your success.

Staff members, you play a vital role in our school family. The connections you build with students are akin to the bonds formed within a family. Your guidance and mentorship shape the future of our students, and in doing so, you become an integral part of their extended family.

Let us not forget that family extends beyond blood relations. The friendships we forge in school become an extended family. The camaraderie and shared experiences among classmates create bonds that last a lifetime. Cherish these friendships, for they are an essential part of your support system.

In a world that sometimes seems to move too fast, let's take a moment to appreciate the moments spent with our families. Engage in conversations, share stories, and create memories that will be cherished for years to come.

As we strive for academic excellence, let us not lose sight of the values instilled by our families. Integrity, compassion, and resilience are qualities that serve as the bedrock of a strong character. Carry these values with you as you navigate the challenges that lie ahead.

In conclusion, I urge each one of you to reflect on the importance of family. Embrace the love and support that surrounds you, both within these school walls and at home. As a school family, let us foster an environment where everyone feels connected, valued, and supported.

Thank you, and let's continue to build a strong, united family here at our beloved school.

54

Justice

Ladies and gentlemen, esteemed faculty, and our bright students,

I stand before you today to delve into a topic that resonates deeply within the core values of our school community - Justice. As we navigate the corridors of education, let us not forget the crucial role that justice plays in shaping our learning environment and the future of our students.

Justice, a word heavy with meaning, transcends mere legality. It encompasses fairness, equity, and the pursuit of what is right. As Nelson Mandela once said, "Education is the most powerful weapon which you can use to change the world." Indeed, it is through education that we instil the principles of justice in our students.

In our classrooms, justice thrives when every student is given an equal opportunity to learn and grow. Let's remember the words of Martin Luther King Jr., who eloquently stated, "Injustice anywhere is a threat to justice everywhere." Our commitment to justice must extend beyond the school gates, fostering a sense of responsibility and empathy that will serve our students well beyond graduation.

To the students, I implore you to be the champions of justice. Maya Angelou once said, "I think we all have empathy. We may not have enough courage to display it." Displaying empathy requires courage - the courage to stand up for what is right, to support your peers, and to challenge injustice wherever it may lurk. Your actions today will shape the world you inherit tomorrow.

Faculty members, you are the architects of justice within our school. Your guidance and mentorship lay the foundation for an equitable and supportive learning environment. Remember the words of Confucius: "To put the world right in order, we must first put the nation in order; to put the nation in order, we must first put the family in order; to put the family in order, we must first cultivate our personal life; we must first set our hearts right."

Let us cultivate our personal commitment to justice, setting our hearts right so that we can impart this essential virtue to the next generation. Justice should not be a distant ideal but a daily practice within the walls of our school.

In conclusion, as we embark on this journey of learning and growth, let us carry with us the profound wisdom of Justice Thurgood Marshall: "In recognizing the humanity of our fellow beings, we pay ourselves the highest tribute." By recognizing and upholding the humanity in each other, we foster a community where justice reigns supreme.

Thank you, and may the pursuit of justice guide our path in education and beyond.

55

Kindness

Ladies and gentlemen, esteemed faculty, and beloved students,

Good [morning/afternoon/evening], and thank you for gathering here today. It is truly an honour to address such a wonderful community that embodies the spirit of our school. Today, I want to talk to you about a simple yet powerful virtue that can transform lives and create a positive ripple effect in our school and beyond - kindness.

As Aesop once said, "No act of kindness, no matter how small, is ever wasted." This timeless wisdom holds true in our daily lives, within the walls of our school and in every interaction we share. Kindness is the currency that enriches the human experience, fostering a sense of unity and compassion.

Let me share a parable with you. There's a tale of a young boy who, upon discovering a wounded bird, chose to nurture it back to health. His act of kindness extended beyond a mere gesture; it represented the inherent goodness within us all. Each of us has the power to be that young boy, mending the wings of others with our words and actions.

In our school, kindness is not just a virtue but a way of life. It manifests in the thoughtful gestures of students helping each other with homework, teachers guiding with patience, and staff members going above and beyond their duties. These acts create an environment where learning flourishes and friendships deepen.

Let me remind you of a quote by Mother Teresa, who said, "Kind words can be short and easy to speak, but their echoes are truly endless." The impact of our words and actions extends far beyond the moment they are uttered or performed. A kind word can uplift a spirit, motivate a friend, or inspire a colleague. It is through these small acts that we shape the collective ethos of our school.

As we navigate the challenges of academics and personal growth, let us be mindful of the impact we can have on each other's lives. It is not always about grand gestures; sometimes, a smile, a helping hand, or a word of encouragement can make a world of difference.

In closing, I want to leave you with a challenge. Let kindness be your compass, guiding your actions and interactions. Remember the parable of the young boy and the wounded bird, and recognize the potential within each of you to make a positive impact. Let our school be a beacon of kindness, where every student, teacher, and staff member contribute to a culture of compassion and support.

Thank you for your attention, and let us continue to build a community where kindness is not just a virtue but a way of life.

56

Sharing

Ladies and gentlemen, esteemed faculty, and our wonderful students,

Today, I would like to address a fundamental value that forms the bedrock of our school community – sharing. As we navigate the corridors of knowledge and growth, it is crucial to recognize the power that lies in sharing, both within our academic endeavours and our interpersonal connections.

Allow me to begin with a poignant quote by Helen Keller: "Alone, we can do so little; together, we can do so much." These words encapsulate the essence of sharing - the understanding that our collective strength far surpasses our individual capabilities. In the context of education, sharing knowledge is a catalyst for intellectual growth. When we share our insights, experiences, and understanding, we create a vibrant tapestry of learning that benefits everyone.

Consider the parable of the Stone Soup, a tale that resonates with the spirit of sharing. In the story, a traveller arrives in a village with nothing but an empty pot. He fills it with water, places a stone in it, and begins to boil it. Intrigued, the villagers inquire about the peculiar soup. The traveller explains that it's stone soup and would be even better with a few additional ingredients. Slowly but surely, each villager contributes something, be it vegetables, herbs, or spices. In the end, they share a delicious, communal feast that was unimaginable when the traveller first arrived.

This parable illustrates the transformative power of sharing. Each person brings their unique contribution, and together they create something greater than the sum of its parts. Similarly, in our academic and social endeavours, every student and staff member have valuable insights and talents to share. Embracing this collective spirit fosters an environment where everyone can thrive.

Sharing extends beyond the realm of knowledge. It encompasses empathy, kindness, and support. As we move through our daily interactions, let us be mindful of the opportunities to share not only information but also encouragement and understanding. A simple act of kindness can have a ripple effect, creating a positive atmosphere that enhances the well-being of our entire community.

In conclusion, let us internalize the wisdom of Helen Keller and the lesson from the Stone Soup parable. Through sharing, we amplify our potential, create a richer learning experience, and build a stronger, more compassionate community. As we journey together in this academic adventure, let sharing be the compass that guides us, making our school a place where each individual flourishes and our collective achievements shine brightly.

Thank you, and may the spirit of sharing continue to illuminate our path towards excellence.

57

Hard Work

Ladies and gentlemen, esteemed faculty, dedicated staff, and our bright students,

Good [morning/afternoon/evening],

It is truly an honour to stand before you today as we delve into a topic that resonates deeply with the essence of our journey - hard work. As we navigate the corridors of knowledge and character-building, let us reflect on the profound words of Thomas Edison: "Genius is one percent inspiration and ninety-nine percent perspiration."

Imagine a world where inspiration alone fuelled our accomplishments. It is a compelling thought, but the reality is that the path to success is paved with the persistent steps of hard work. Our school is a crucible of learning, and within these walls, the alchemy of effort transforms dreams into tangible achievements.

In the spirit of imparting wisdom, let me share a parable that underscores the significance of hard work. There once was a diligent ant who toiled tirelessly, preparing for the inevitable winter. Meanwhile, a carefree grasshopper sang away the warm days without a care for the future. When winter arrived, the ant thrived with abundance, while the grasshopper faced the harsh reality of unpreparedness. This fable serves as a timeless reminder that diligence and hard work are the cornerstones of prosperity.

Our students, you are the architects of your destinies. As you sit in classrooms, absorb knowledge, and tackle challenges, remember the words of Vince Lombardi: "The only place success comes before work is in the dictionary." Your academic journey is a testament to your commitment, and each lesson, assignment, and exam is a brick in the foundation of your future success.

To the dedicated staff and faculty, your unwavering commitment to nurturing these young minds is commendable. Your hard work in crafting an environment of learning excellence does not go unnoticed. It is through your dedication that our students are inspired to embrace the values of tenacity and diligence.

As we celebrate the achievements within our school, let us recognize that the road to success is not always smooth. There will be obstacles, setbacks, and moments of self-doubt. However, it is in these challenging times that the true essence of hard work shines. The late basketball legend Michael Jordan once said, "I've missed more than 9,000 shots in my career. I've lost almost 300 games. Twenty-six times, I've been trusted to take the game-winning shot and missed. I've failed over and over and over again in my life. And that is why I succeed."

In closing, let us embrace the ethos of hard work as the catalyst for our collective success. Whether student or staff, let us be like the ant, diligently preparing for the challenges that lie ahead. As we move forward, let the legacy of our efforts be a testament to the enduring power of hard work.

Thank you for your attention, and may our journey continue to be one marked by diligence, perseverance, and ultimate success.

58

Moral Compass

Ladies and gentlemen, esteemed faculty, and cherished students,

Today, I stand before you to discuss a topic that is the guiding force behind our actions, decisions, and the very essence of our character - the moral compass. As we navigate through the seas of education and life, it is crucial to ensure that our moral compass remains true and unwavering.

Allow me to begin with a profound quote from Mahatma Gandhi, who said, "You must be the change you want to see in the world." These words encapsulate the essence of our discussion today. Our moral compass directs us not only to recognize what is right and wrong but also compels us to embody those values.

In a world filled with diverse perspectives, it becomes increasingly important to hold onto a moral foundation that transcends cultural and societal boundaries. Let me share a parable with you - the story of the Good

Samaritan. This tale reminds us that compassion knows no limits, and our moral compass should guide us to help those in need, irrespective of differences.

As we journey through the corridors of this institution, let us reflect on our actions and choices. Are we, as educators and students, fostering an environment where integrity, empathy, and kindness prevail? The choices we make daily shape not only our individual character but also the collective ethos of our school community.

Let me leave you with another quote, this time from the great Martin Luther King Jr., who proclaimed, "The time is always right to do what is right." This echoes the idea that our moral compass is not a stagnant entity but a dynamic force that calls us to act with righteousness in every moment.

In conclusion, let us strive to cultivate and preserve a moral compass that points us towards the path of virtue. As educators, instil these values in our students, and as students, carry them forward into the broader world. Together, let us create a legacy of ethical conduct, empathy, and understanding that will endure far beyond our time within these walls.

Thank you for your attention, and may our moral compass guide us on this shared journey of growth and enlightenment.

59

Personal Values

Ladies and gentlemen, esteemed faculty, and cherished students,

Good [morning/afternoon/evening],

Today, I want to talk to you about something that shapes our character, guides our actions, and defines who we are as individuals – our personal values. These values are the compass that directs us in our journey through life, influencing the decisions we make and the paths we choose.

As renowned author and speaker, Jim Rohn, once said, "Your values are the foundation of your personal character. They shape who you are and who you are becoming." This quote serves as a reminder that our values not only reflect who we are now but also play a crucial role in shaping our future selves.

Let me share with you a parable that resonates deeply with the essence of personal values. It's the story of "The Two Wolves." An old Cherokee is teaching his grandson about life. He says, "A fight is going on inside me. It's a terrible fight between two wolves. One represents fear, anger, envy, sorrow, regret, greed, arrogance, self-pity, guilt, resentment, inferiority, lies, false pride, superiority, and ego. The other stands for joy, peace, love, hope, serenity, humility, kindness, benevolence, empathy, generosity, truth, compassion, and faith."

The young boy pauses, absorbing the wisdom, before asking, "Which wolf will win, Grandfather?" The wise elder responds, "The one you feed."

This parable beautifully illustrates the constant internal struggle between positive and negative values. It challenges us to be mindful of the values we nourish within ourselves, recognizing that our actions and attitudes are shaped by the wolf we choose to feed.

In the fast-paced world we live in, where external pressures often vie for our attention, it becomes essential to anchor ourselves in our personal values. They serve as our moral compass, guiding us through the storms and challenges life throws our way. As the great Mahatma Gandhi once said, "Your beliefs become your thoughts, your thoughts become your words, your words become your actions, your actions become your habits, your habits become your values, and your values become your destiny."

Our school community is a tapestry woven from the individual threads of each student and staff member. The strength of this community lies in the shared values that bind us together. Let us cultivate a culture where respect, integrity, compassion, and responsibility are not just words but lived principles that shape our interactions and collaborations.

As we navigate through our academic and personal journeys, let us be conscious of the values we embody and uphold. Let them be the lighthouse guiding us, ensuring that our choices align with the principles we hold dear.

In conclusion, remember the power of your personal values. Embrace them, nurture them, and let them be the guiding force in your journey of self-discovery and growth. As we foster a community built on strong values, we contribute not only to our individual success but also to the collective strength of our school.

Thank you for your attention, and may your personal values illuminate the path ahead.

60

Building Character

Ladies and gentlemen, esteemed faculty, and cherished students,

Good [morning/afternoon/evening],

It is with great pleasure and a sense of profound responsibility that I stand before you today to discuss a topic that is fundamental to our school's ethos – building character. In the words of the renowned author and speaker Zig Ziglar, "Your attitude, not your aptitude, will determine your altitude."

As we navigate the rich tapestry of education, it is crucial to recognize that academic achievements, while vital, only scratch the surface of true success. Our character, the essence of who we are, serves as the compass guiding us through the journey of life. And so, I implore each of you to invest in the construction of a character so robust that it withstands the tests of time.

Allow me to share a parable that encapsulates the essence of character-building. It's the tale of the two builders. One constructed a house upon the shifting sands, solely focused on appearances and expedience. The other painstakingly built on a foundation of solid rock, considering the long-term durability of the structure. When the storms of life came, only the house with a strong foundation weathered the challenges. So too must we fortify our characters to withstand the tempests that life may throw our way.

The journey of character-building is intricately tied to the values we embrace. A wise man once said, "Watch your thoughts, they become your words; watch your words, they become your actions; watch your actions, they become your habits; watch your habits, they become your character; watch your character, for it becomes your destiny." Let us be vigilant custodians of our thoughts, for they mould the very fabric of our character.

In the spirit of camaraderie and mutual support, let us also heed the words of Helen Keller, who stated, "Alone, we can do so little; together, we can do so much." Our school community is a microcosm of society, and it is within these walls that we learn to appreciate the strengths and virtues of our fellow students and staff. Let us foster an environment where empathy, kindness, and respect are the cornerstones upon which we build our collective character.

As we strive for academic excellence, let us not forget that true success lies not just in what we achieve but, in the person, we become along the way. Maya Angelou's words echo this sentiment: "Success is liking yourself, liking what you do, and liking how you do it."

In conclusion, my dear students and esteemed staff, let us embark on this collective journey of character-building with enthusiasm and purpose. Remember, it is not the destination that defines us but the path we take and the character we develop along the way.

Thank you, and may the foundation of your character be as unyielding as the rock upon which we build our dreams.

Environmental Education

Ladies and gentlemen, esteemed faculty, and our wonderful students,

I stand before you today with a sense of urgency and responsibility, as we delve into a topic that is not just relevant but imperative for the well-being of our planet – environmental education.

As the great conservationist Baba Dioum once said, "In the end, we will conserve only what we love; we will love only what we understand, and we will understand only what we are taught." These words resonate with the core of why we, as an educational institution, need to prioritize environmental education.

Our world is facing unprecedented environmental challenges - climate change, deforestation, pollution, and loss of biodiversity. It is our duty to equip our students with the knowledge and understanding necessary to be stewards of the environment. Environmental education is not a choice; it is a fundamental part of preparing our students for the future.

Rachel Carson, the influential marine biologist and author, once remarked, "The more clearly we can focus our attention on the wonders and realities of the universe about us, the less taste we shall have for destruction." Through environmental education, we open the door to these wonders, fostering a deep appreciation for the intricate balance of nature and a commitment to preserving it.

Our curriculum must embrace interdisciplinary approaches, weaving environmental themes into various subjects. Let us not forget the wise words of Margaret Mead, who said, "Children must be taught how to think, not what to think." We aim to cultivate critical thinkers who understand the interconnectedness of human actions and their impact on the environment.

As a school community, we must lead by example. Mahatma Gandhi once said, "Be the change that you wish to see in the world." Let our campus be a living testament to sustainability and eco-conscious practices. From waste reduction to energy conservation, let us instil in our students the values of environmental stewardship.

Furthermore, we must forge partnerships with local environmental organizations, inviting experts to share their knowledge and experiences. In the words of David Orr, "All education is environmental education." Every lesson, every field trip, and every project should contribute to a holistic understanding of our role in preserving the planet.

In conclusion, let us remember the timeless words of Chief Seattle, "We do not inherit the earth from our ancestors; we borrow it from our children." It is our collective responsibility to ensure that we return a thriving and sustainable planet to the generations that follow.

Thank you for your commitment to environmental education. Together, we can inspire a generation that not only learns about the environment but actively participates in its preservation.

62

The Value of Education

Ladies and gentlemen, esteemed faculty, dedicated staff, and our cherished students,

I stand before you today with a profound sense of pride and gratitude as we reflect on the enduring value of education. In these pivotal moments, let us delve into the essence of why education remains the cornerstone of our lives and the bedrock of our society.

Education is not merely the acquisition of facts and figures, but a transformative journey that empowers individuals to navigate the complexities of the world. It opens doors to new perspectives, broadens horizons, and cultivates the critical thinking skills essential for success in our ever-evolving global landscape.

As educators, we bear the responsibility of shaping not only informed minds but compassionate hearts. Our classrooms are crucibles where character is forged, empathy is nurtured, and values are instilled. It is here that seeds of curiosity are planted, sparking a lifelong thirst for knowledge.

To our students, I implore you to embrace the gift of education with unwavering enthusiasm. Recognize that learning extends far beyond the confines of textbooks-it encompasses the lessons embedded in every challenge, triumph, and interaction. Your education is a passport to a future of endless possibilities; wield it wisely.

For our dedicated staff, you are the architects of dreams, the catalysts of change. Your commitment to fostering an environment that nurtures intellectual curiosity and personal growth is commendable. Together, let us continue to foster a culture of lifelong learning, where both students and educators are inspired to reach new heights.

In a world grappling with myriad challenges, education stands as a beacon of hope. It is the tool that empowers individuals to break the shackles of ignorance and prejudice. Let us cultivate a community where the pursuit of knowledge is not a mere obligation but a shared passion.

As we navigate the vast ocean of information, let us equip ourselves with the discernment to separate the profound from the superficial, the meaningful from the trivial. In doing so, we fortify our minds against the tides of misinformation and empower ourselves as responsible citizens.

In conclusion, the value of education is immeasurable. It is a catalyst for personal growth, societal progress, and global harmony. As we continue this journey together, let us remain steadfast in our commitment to fostering a community where education is not just a means to an end but a lifelong companion.

Thank you, and may our pursuit of knowledge be both enlightening and enriching.

63

Critical Thinking

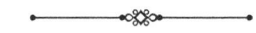

Ladies and gentlemen, esteemed faculty, dedicated staff, and our brilliant students,

Good [morning/afternoon/evening], it is truly an honour to stand before you today as we delve into a topic that is not just essential for academic success but is a cornerstone of lifelong learning – critical thinking.

In the fast-paced world we live in, where information bombards us from all directions, the ability to think critically becomes paramount. Critical thinking is not merely about memorizing facts; it's about questioning, analysing, and synthesizing information. It's the tool that empowers us to navigate the complexities of the world with discernment and clarity.

As educators, our goal extends beyond the transmission of knowledge; we aim to cultivate independent thinkers, problem solvers, and individuals capable of making informed decisions. Critical thinking is the catalyst that transforms information into understanding and mere knowledge into wisdom.

To our students, I implore you to embrace the challenge of thinking critically. Question assumptions, explore diverse perspectives, and seek evidence. Remember, true understanding often lies in the space between certainty and doubt. The classroom is your training ground for these intellectual pursuits, preparing you not just for exams but for the dynamic challenges life presents.

To our esteemed faculty and staff, your role is pivotal. Nurture an environment that fosters curiosity and encourages students to express their thoughts. Challenge them to think beyond the textbooks, sparking discussions that ignite intellectual curiosity. Our duty is not only to teach subjects but to instil in our students the ability to think for themselves.

Let us also acknowledge the importance of modelling critical thinking. As educators, administrators, and leaders, we must embody the principles we advocate. Demonstrating thoughtful decision-making and an openness to new ideas sets a powerful example for our students.

In conclusion, critical thinking is not a skill limited to the walls of academia; it is a life skill. It equips us to face the unknown, adapt to change, and contribute meaningfully to society. Let us, as a school community, commit ourselves to fostering an atmosphere where critical thinking thrives, where questions are welcomed, and where the pursuit of knowledge is a journey of discovery.

Thank you for your attention, and let us continue to cultivate minds that not only absorb information but also critically engage with the world around them.

64

Democratic Education

Ladies and gentlemen, esteemed faculty, and dear students,

I stand before you today to discuss a crucial aspect of our educational philosophy: democratic education. Our commitment to fostering an environment that values inclusivity, collaboration, and respect is what sets our institution apart.

In a democratic education system, every voice matters. It's about empowering each student to actively participate in shaping their learning experience. Here, we believe that education is not a one-size-fits-all concept. Instead, it's a dynamic process where students are encouraged to express their ideas, ask questions, and engage in meaningful dialogue.

Our classrooms are not just spaces for lectures but platforms for discussion. Teachers are facilitators, guiding students to think critically and encouraging them to explore diverse perspectives. By embracing democratic principles, we are preparing our students not just for exams but for life beyond these walls.

Furthermore, our commitment extends to the staff. A democratic education system values the input of educators, recognizing their expertise and unique insights. Collaboration between teachers, administration, and staff ensures a holistic approach to education, one that nurtures the growth of the entire school community.

In this democratic spirit, we encourage students to take on leadership roles through student councils and involvement in decision-making processes. This builds a sense of responsibility and ownership, fostering a community where everyone has a stake in the success of our school.

However, with this empowerment comes the responsibility to respect the opinions and ideas of others. Our commitment to democratic education is also a commitment to cultivating a culture of mutual understanding and tolerance. It's about teaching our students not only what to think but how to think, promoting empathy and open-mindedness.

In conclusion, our dedication to democratic education goes beyond the classroom. It's a philosophy that shapes the very foundation of our school. As we continue on this journey, let us remember that the strength of our community lies in the diversity of thought and the power of collaboration.

Thank you for your attention, and let us continue to build an educational environment where every voice is heard, and every individual has the opportunity to thrive.

65

Empathy

Ladies and gentlemen, esteemed faculty, and dear students,

Good [morning/afternoon/evening], I stand before you today to discuss a topic that is not just a virtue but a cornerstone of our shared humanity - empathy.

As we navigate the halls of this institution, it is crucial to remember that each person carries a unique story. Empathy is the compass that helps us understand those stories, fostering a sense of understanding, compassion, and unity.

Allow me to share a quote by the renowned author J.K. Rowling: "Understanding is the first step to acceptance, and only with acceptance can there be recovery." These words resonate deeply with the essence of empathy. To truly embrace the diversity within our school, we must strive to understand one another.

I'd like to draw inspiration from a parable that has withstood the test of time. The tale of "The Good

Samaritan" teaches us about compassion and empathy. In a world where we are constantly bombarded with differences, the Good Samaritan serves as a timeless reminder that empathy knows no boundaries. It is an act of kindness that transcends societal norms and embraces the common thread of humanity.

In the realm of education, empathy becomes a powerful tool. Teachers, you play a pivotal role in shaping the minds of our students. The ability to empathize with each student's unique challenges and strengths not only fosters a positive learning environment but also instils values that extend far beyond the classroom.

Students, your journey within these walls is not solely about academic achievement but also about personal growth. Empathy is a skill that will serve you well in the classroom and beyond. As you interact with your peers, remember that kindness and understanding can create a ripple effect, making our school a nurturing space for everyone.

In conclusion, let us embrace empathy as a guiding principle in our daily interactions. As we seek to understand one another, we strengthen the bonds that make our school a community of compassion. Remember, empathy is not just a virtue; it's a force that has the power to transform lives.

Thank you for your attention, and may empathy guide our actions and interactions every day.

66

Equality

Ladies and gentlemen, esteemed faculty, and our bright students,

Good [morning/afternoon/evening], it is an honour to stand before you today to address a topic of utmost importance - Equality. In the diverse tapestry of our school community, the concept of equality is not just a principle; it is a guiding light that shapes our shared journey.

As Nelson Mandela once said, "Education is the most powerful weapon which you can use to change the world." Our commitment to equality begins right here, in these classrooms and hallways where knowledge is not just a privilege but a right for every student. Each of you brings unique perspectives and talents, and it's through equality that we harness the power of diversity.

Let me share a parable that resonates with the essence of equality. Imagine a vast forest where trees of different species coexist. Each tree, regardless of its size or type, contributes to the forest's beauty and balance. In our school, each student is like a unique tree, contributing to the richness of our academic ecosystem. It's in recognizing and valuing these differences that we find strength and unity.

Equality, however, extends beyond our student body. Our dedicated staff plays a crucial role in fostering an environment where everyone is seen, heard, and valued. Maya Angelou once said, "We all should know that diversity makes for a rich tapestry, and we must understand that all the threads of the tapestry are equal in value no matter their colour." In the intricate tapestry of our school, each staff member weaves a thread, contributing to the vibrant narrative of equality.

Yet, embracing equality is an ongoing journey, not a destination. It requires continuous introspection and a commitment to dismantling barriers. It's about providing equal opportunities, irrespective of background or circumstances. As Martin Luther King Jr. profoundly stated, "I have a dream that my four little children will one day live in a nation where they will not be judged by the colour of their skin but by the content of their character." Our commitment is to create an environment where every student and staff member is judged by their character, potential, and contributions.

To achieve this vision, we must cultivate empathy and understanding. Engage in open conversations, listen to one another, and embrace the strength that comes from unity in diversity. Our differences are not obstacles; they are assets that enrich our learning community.

In conclusion, let us remember that equality is not just a concept but a lived reality within our school. It's a commitment to fostering an environment where each individual has the opportunity to thrive and contribute their unique strengths to the collective growth of our community.

Thank you for your attention, and may we continue this journey of equality hand in hand, creating a legacy that echoes through the halls of our school for generations to come.

Health Education

Ladies and gentlemen, esteemed faculty, and dear students,

Good [morning/afternoon/evening],

I stand before you today to emphasize the crucial importance of health education in our school community. Our commitment to nurturing not only academic excellence but also the overall well-being of our students is unwavering. As we embark on this journey together, let us recognize that a healthy mind and body are the foundation for success.

Health education extends beyond textbooks and classrooms; it's a holistic approach that empowers each one of us to make informed decisions about our well-being. Our goal is not only to produce bright minds but to cultivate individuals who understand the significance of a healthy lifestyle.

Firstly, let's address the importance of physical health. Regular exercise is not just a way to stay fit; it contributes to improved concentration, better mood, and overall enhanced academic performance. I encourage both students and staff to incorporate physical activities into their daily routines, whether it's a brisk walk, a workout, or engaging in sports.

Equally vital is mental health. In a world filled with constant challenges, it is imperative that we prioritize mental well-being. Our school is committed to providing resources and support systems to help manage stress and foster a positive environment. Let us break the stigma surrounding mental health and encourage open conversations within our school community.

Nutrition plays a pivotal role in our overall health. As responsible individuals, we should be mindful of what we consume. A balanced diet not only fuels our bodies but also influences our cognitive functions. Let us make informed choices about the food we eat, promoting a culture of health-consciousness among our peers and colleagues.

Furthermore, we must address the significance of preventive healthcare. Regular check-ups and health screenings can detect potential issues early, allowing for timely intervention. I encourage everyone to take advantage of the health resources available to us, ensuring that we are proactive in maintaining our well-being.

In conclusion, health education is not just a subject; it's a life skill. It equips us with the knowledge to lead fulfilling and healthy lives. I urge each member of our school community to embrace this holistic approach to education, for a healthy mind and body pave the way for a bright and successful future.

Thank you for your attention, and let us work together to foster a culture of well-being within our school.

Moral Development

Ladies and gentlemen, esteemed faculty, and dear students,

Good [morning/afternoon/evening],

I stand before you today to address a topic of utmost importance in our educational journey - moral development. As we navigate the corridors of academia, it is crucial that we recognize the significance of shaping not just bright minds but nurturing compassionate hearts.

In the fast-paced world we live in, where technological advancements abound, it is easy to lose sight of the fundamental values that form the bedrock of a strong society. Today, I want to emphasize the pivotal role our school plays in fostering the moral development of our students.

Firstly, let us acknowledge that moral development is a lifelong journey. It begins here, within the walls of our school, where our students are not merely recipients of knowledge but contributors to a culture of empathy, integrity, and kindness. Each interaction, each decision, becomes a building block in their character formation.

Our dedicated educators are not just disseminators of information; they are the architects of moral growth. Through their guidance, students learn the importance of honesty, responsibility, and respect. It is not just about acing exams but about excelling as compassionate individuals who contribute positively to their communities.

Moreover, our commitment to moral development extends beyond the classroom. Extracurricular activities, community service projects, and collaborative initiatives are avenues for students to apply ethical principles in real-world situations. These experiences instil a sense of social responsibility and empathy, fostering a well-rounded and morally conscious individual.

As we nurture moral development, it is imperative that we create an environment where students feel safe to explore their values and question the world around them. Encouraging open dialogue, embracing diversity, and cultivating a culture of inclusivity are essential components in this journey.

Parents, you are integral partners in this endeavour. The values we instil in our students at school must find resonance at home. The collaboration between school and home amplifies the impact of moral teachings, reinforcing a consistent message that shapes the character of our young learners.

In conclusion, let us remain steadfast in our commitment to moral development. Our school is not just a place of academic excellence; it is a crucible where character is forged. As we prepare our students for the challenges that lie ahead, let us equip them not just with knowledge but with the moral compass that will guide them towards a future of integrity, compassion, and positive impact.

Thank you for your attention, and let us continue this journey of moral development hand in hand.

Social Education

Ladies and gentlemen, esteemed staff, and cherished students,

I stand before you today with a profound sense of responsibility and excitement to discuss a topic that is not only pertinent but also pivotal in shaping our society - social education. As Nelson Mandela once said, "Education is the most powerful weapon which you can use to change the world." And indeed, social education is the cornerstone of this transformative power.

In a world increasingly interconnected yet paradoxically fragmented, the importance of social education cannot be overstated. It encompasses a wide array of skills and values, from empathy and communication to critical thinking and cultural competence. It is the bedrock upon which we build a society characterized by understanding, tolerance, and respect.

As members of this educational community, we have a duty not only to impart academic knowledge but also to cultivate the social and emotional intelligence that is essential for navigating the complexities of human interaction. Just as we teach mathematics and science, so too must we teach kindness and compassion.

To quote the renowned educator, Horace Mann, "Education then, beyond all other devices of human origin, is the great equalizer of the conditions of men." Yet, true equality cannot be achieved without addressing the social injustices that persist in our world. It is through social education that we empower our students to become advocates for change, to challenge prejudice and discrimination wherever they encounter it.

But social education is not confined to the classroom. It extends beyond the walls of our school and into the fabric of our community. It is in our everyday interactions, our shared experiences, and our collective efforts to build a more inclusive and equitable society.

Today, I urge each and every one of you to embrace the principles of social education in your daily lives. Seek to understand perspectives that differ from your own. Stand up against injustice, even when it is inconvenient. And above all, treat others with the dignity and respect that every human being deserves.

In closing, let me leave you with the words of Malala Yousafzai, a beacon of courage and resilience in the face of adversity: "Let us remember: One book, one pen, one child, and one teacher can change the world." Together, let us harness the power of social education to create a world that is fairer, kinder, and more compassionate for all.

Thank you

70

Spiritual Education

Ladies and gentlemen, esteemed students, and cherished staff,

As we gather here today, I'm reminded of the words of Albert Einstein who said, "Education is not the learning of facts, but the training of the mind to think." Today, I want to talk to you about a dimension of education that goes beyond the textbooks and the exams. I want to talk about spiritual education.

Now, before you start picturing monks meditating in the classrooms, let me clarify what I mean by spiritual education. It's about nurturing the soul, fostering empathy, compassion, and a sense of interconnectedness with the world around us. It's about finding purpose and meaning beyond material success. And it's about recognizing the importance of values like honesty, integrity, and kindness in shaping our lives.

In a world that's increasingly fast-paced and competitive, it's easy to lose sight of these fundamental aspects of our humanity. But it's precisely in times like these that spiritual education becomes even more important. It's the anchor that keeps us grounded amidst the storms of life.

Now, I'm not suggesting that we turn our school into a temple or a church. But I do believe that we can infuse spiritual values into every aspect of our education. Whether it's through literature that inspires empathy, discussions that encourage critical thinking and reflection, or acts of service that remind us of the joy of giving, there are countless ways to cultivate the spiritual dimension of our lives.

And let's not forget the role of humour in all of this. As Mark Twain once said, "Humour is the great thing, the saving thing after all. The minute it crops up, all our hardnesses yield, all our irritations, and resentments flit away, and a sunny spirit takes their place." So, let's not take ourselves too seriously as we embark on this journey of spiritual education. Let's laugh together, learn together, and grow together as a community.

In closing, I want to leave you with a quote from the Dalai Lama, who said, "The purpose of our lives is to be happy." And I truly believe that spiritual education is the key to unlocking that happiness. So, let's embrace it wholeheartedly, let's nurture our souls, and let's make our school a beacon of light in an often dark and chaotic world.

*** Thank you ***

71

Sympathy

Ladies and gentlemen, esteemed faculty members, and beloved students,

Today, I stand before you to delve into a topic that is not often discussed in the corridors of academia but is nonetheless fundamental to our humanity: sympathy. As we navigate our academic and personal journeys, it is imperative that we cultivate a deep sense of empathy and understanding towards one another.

Sympathy, as the great philosopher Voltaire once said, "is a sentiment that should precede all others; a kind of universal bond of society, and the foundation of all the virtues." It is this sentiment that forms the bedrock of our school community, fostering an environment where kindness, compassion, and understanding thrive.

Imagine, if you will, a parable:

In a bustling marketplace, there lived a merchant renowned for his wealth and success. One day, as he walked through the crowded streets, he stumbled upon a beggar huddled in a corner, shivering from the cold. The merchant, accustomed to the luxuries of his life, could have easily passed by without a second glance. But something stirred within him - a spark of sympathy. He approached the beggar, offering him his cloak and a warm meal.

In that simple act of kindness, the merchant exemplified the power of sympathy. He recognized the humanity in the beggar, transcending barriers of wealth and status. This parable serves as a poignant reminder that empathy knows no bounds - it is a force capable of bridging the gaps between us, forging connections that transcend our differences.

As members of this school community, we are bound together by a shared purpose - to learn, to grow, and to support one another along the way. In times of triumph, let us celebrate together. In moments of struggle, let us extend a helping hand. Let us cultivate a culture of empathy and understanding, where every voice is heard and every heart is valued.

But sympathy is not merely a passive emotion - it is a call to action. It compels us to step outside of ourselves, to walk in another's shoes, and to advocate for those who may not have a voice. Whether it be lending a listening ear to a friend in need or standing up against injustice in our community, let us embody the spirit of sympathy in all that we do.

In closing, I leave you with the words of Mother Teresa: "I alone cannot change the world, but I can cast a stone across the waters to create many ripples." Each act of sympathy, no matter how small, has the power to create a ripple effect, inspiring others to follow suit.

So let us embark on this journey together - a journey fuelled by compassion, guided by empathy, and enriched by the bonds of sympathy. For it is in embracing our shared humanity that we truly fulfil the promise of education - to nurture not only the mind, but also the heart.

*** Thank you ***

International Day of Education (January 24)

Good morning, students and staff,

As we gather here today, I am reminded of the profound words of Nelson Mandela: "Education is the most powerful weapon which you can use to change the world." On this International Education Day, we come together to celebrate the transformative power of education and the rich tapestry of history that has shaped our world.

History is not just a subject confined to textbooks; it is a living, breathing narrative that informs our present and guides our future. It teaches us about the triumphs and struggles of humanity, the mistakes of the past, and the potential for a brighter tomorrow. By understanding where we come from, we gain insight into who we are and where we are headed.

Today, as we reflect on the importance of history, let us also recognize the diversity of experiences and perspectives that make up our global community. International Education Day serves as a reminder that education knows no boundaries - it is a fundamental human right that should be accessible to all, regardless of nationality, ethnicity, or socioeconomic status.

So how can we celebrate International Education Day in meaningful ways? Here are a few suggestions:

Embrace Diversity: Take this opportunity to learn about different cultures, traditions, and viewpoints. Host cultural exchange events, guest speakers, or film screenings that highlight the richness of our global heritage.

Foster Dialogue: Encourage open and respectful discussions about history, politics, and current events. Provide platforms for students and staff to share their perspectives and engage in constructive debate.

Volunteer and Give Back: Education is not just about acquiring knowledge; it is also about using that knowledge to make a positive impact on the world. Organize community service projects, fundraisers, or awareness campaigns to support educational initiatives locally and globally.

Reflect and Reimagine: Use this day as an opportunity to reflect on our own educational journey and how we can continue to grow and evolve as learners. Encourage innovation and creativity in teaching and learning, and explore new ways to make education more inclusive and accessible for all.

As we embark on this journey of celebration and exploration, let us remember that education is not a destination but a lifelong pursuit. It is through learning and understanding that we can build a more just, equitable, and compassionate world for ourselves and future generations.

Thank you for joining me in commemorating International Education Day. Together, let us continue to strive for excellence, embrace diversity, and uphold the values of knowledge, understanding, and solidarity.

Have a wonderful day ahead.

International Day of Clean Energy (January 26)

Dear Students and Staff,

Today, I stand before you to shed light on a topic of utmost significance - the International Day of Clean Energy. As we embark on this journey of awareness and action, it is imperative to understand the history, importance, and ways to celebrate this pivotal day.

The International Day of Clean Energy, celebrated annually on 26th January, serves as a global platform to advocate for sustainable energy practices and raise awareness about the importance of transitioning to cleaner, renewable energy sources. This day was established by the United Nations to emphasize the critical role that clean energy plays in combating climate change, promoting economic growth, and ensuring a sustainable future for generations to come.

Now more than ever, we are witnessing the devastating effects of climate change, from extreme weather events to rising sea levels. It is clear that urgent action is needed to mitigate these impacts and safeguard our planet. Clean energy presents a viable solution to this pressing challenge, offering a sustainable alternative to fossil fuels and reducing greenhouse gas emissions.

As members of our school community, it is our responsibility to not only recognize the importance of clean energy but also to take proactive steps towards its adoption. There are several ways in which we can celebrate the International Day of Clean Energy and contribute to the global effort:

Education and Awareness: We can organize workshops, seminars, and educational campaigns to inform our peers about the benefits of clean energy and the role they can play in promoting its adoption.

Advocacy and Policy: We can advocate for policies that support clean energy initiatives at the local, national, and international levels. By voicing our concerns and demanding action, we can influence decision-makers to prioritize renewable energy development.

Community Engagement: We can engage with our local community to promote clean energy projects, such as solar panel installations or energy-efficient initiatives. By working together, we can create a more sustainable future for our community and beyond.

Personal Action: We can take individual actions to reduce our carbon footprint and promote clean energy usage in our daily lives. This can include conserving energy, using public transportation, and supporting renewable energy companies.

In celebrating the International Day of Clean Energy, let us reaffirm our commitment to sustainability and environmental stewardship. Together, we have the power to drive positive change and create a cleaner, greener world for future generations.

Thank you for your attention, and let us all strive to make every day a clean energy day.

74

International Day of Human Fraternity 04 February

Ladies and gentlemen, esteemed faculty members, and dear students,

Today, we gather to celebrate an incredibly significant occasion, the International Day of Human Fraternity, observed every 4th of February. This day holds profound importance in reminding us of the values of tolerance, solidarity, and peaceful coexistence among all people, regardless of race, religion, or nationality.

The history behind this day dates back to 2019 when the United Nations General Assembly adopted a resolution to proclaim February 4th as the International Day of Human Fraternity. This decision was inspired by the historic Document on Human Fraternity for World Peace and Living Together, signed by Pope Francis and the Grand Imam of Al-Azhar, Sheikh Ahmed el-Tayeb, in Abu Dhabi in 2019. This document calls for mutual understanding and respect among people of different faiths and backgrounds, emphasizing the importance of dialogue and cooperation in building a more peaceful and inclusive world.

As we commemorate this day, it's essential to reflect on how we can contribute to promoting human fraternity in our own lives and communities. Here are some ways we can do so:

Promoting Understanding and Respect: We must strive to understand and respect the beliefs, cultures, and traditions of others, fostering an environment of acceptance and inclusion within our school and beyond.

Fostering Dialogue: Engaging in open and meaningful dialogue allows us to bridge divides, break down stereotypes, and build connections based on mutual respect and empathy.

Acts of Kindness and Service: Small acts of kindness can have a significant impact on promoting harmony and goodwill. Whether it's volunteering in our community or simply extending a helping hand to a classmate in need, every gesture counts.

Educating Ourselves: We must continuously educate ourselves about the diverse perspectives and experiences of people around the world, challenging our own biases and assumptions to promote a more just and equitable society.

Advocating for Peace: Lastly, we must advocate for peace and justice in our world, standing up against discrimination, hatred, and violence wherever they may occur.

In the words of Mahatma Gandhi, "Be the change that you wish to see in the world." Let us strive to embody the principles of human fraternity in our daily lives, creating a more harmonious and compassionate world for ourselves and future generations.

Today, as we come together to celebrate the International Day of Human Fraternity, let us reaffirm our commitment to building a world where all individuals are treated with dignity and respect, where diversity is celebrated, and where peace and understanding prevail.

Thank you

World Day of Social Justice
20 February

Good morning, esteemed students and staff,

As we gather here today, it is with great pleasure and a sense of responsibility that I address you on the occasion of the International Day of Social Justice, observed annually on February 20th. This day serves as a reminder of our collective duty to promote equality, justice, and the well-being of all individuals regardless of race, gender, religion, or socioeconomic status.

The roots of this day trace back to the World Summit for Social Development held in Copenhagen in 1995, where governments committed to the pursuit of social justice for all. Since then, this day has become an opportunity for nations, organizations, and communities worldwide to reflect on progress made and challenges that still lie ahead in achieving social justice.

Social justice is not just a lofty ideal; it is a fundamental principle that underpins the fabric of our society. It is about ensuring that every individual has access to basic human rights, opportunities, and resources necessary to lead a dignified life. It's about standing up against discrimination, inequality, and injustice in all its forms.

As members of this school community, we have a crucial role to play in advancing social justice both within our walls and beyond. We must strive to create an inclusive and respectful environment where diversity is celebrated, and everyone feels valued and respected. We must educate ourselves and others about the root causes of social injustice and work towards dismantling systemic barriers that perpetuate inequality.

There are numerous ways we can celebrate this day and contribute to the cause of social justice. We can organize awareness campaigns, discussions, and workshops to deepen our understanding of social issues and brainstorm solutions. We can engage in acts of kindness and solidarity, reaching out to those in need and advocating for those whose voices are often marginalized.

Let us also take this opportunity to reflect on the lessons that social justice teaches us. It teaches us empathy and compassion, reminding us to always consider the needs and experiences of others. It teaches us courage, urging us to speak out against injustice even when it may be uncomfortable or unpopular. And it teaches us resilience, as we continue to strive for a more just and equitable world despite the challenges we may face.

In the words of Martin Luther King Jr., "Injustice anywhere is a threat to justice everywhere." Let us heed these words and commit ourselves to the pursuit of social justice not just today but every day. Together, we can create a world where every individual is treated with dignity and respect, and where justice truly prevails.

Thank you for your attention, and let us continue this important work together.

World Wildlife Day
03 March

Ladies and gentlemen, esteemed students and staff,

As we gather here today, on this auspicious occasion of International World Wildlife Day, I am filled with a sense of reverence and responsibility towards our planet's precious biodiversity. It is a day where we come together to celebrate the incredible richness of life that surrounds us and reflect on our role in its preservation.

As the renowned conservationist, Jane Goodall, once said, "The least I can do is speak out for those who cannot speak for themselves." Today, let us heed her words and raise our voices for the voiceless creatures with whom we share this planet.

History reminds us of the significance of this day. On March 3rd, 1973, the Convention on International Trade in Endangered Species of Wild Fauna and Flora (CITES) was signed, marking a pivotal moment in global efforts to protect wildlife. Since then, World Wildlife Day has been observed annually to raise awareness about the importance of wildlife conservation.

Now, how can we celebrate this day in meaningful ways? One way is through education. We must educate ourselves and others about the threats facing wildlife, whether it be habitat destruction, poaching, or climate change. Knowledge is power, and through understanding, we can empower ourselves to take action.

Another way to celebrate is through advocacy. We can advocate for policies and practices that promote conservation and sustainability. By raising awareness in our communities and lobbying decision-makers, we can make a tangible difference in the protection of wildlife.

But perhaps the most profound way to celebrate World Wildlife Day is through action. Each one of us has a role to play in preserving our natural world. Whether it's reducing our carbon footprint, supporting conservation organizations, or volunteering our time to protect habitats, every action counts.

As Mahatma Gandhi famously said, "The greatness of a nation and its moral progress can be judged by the way its animals are treated." Let us strive to be a nation, a community, that values and respects all forms of life.

In conclusion, let us remember that we are not separate from nature, but rather, deeply interconnected with it. On this World Wildlife Day, let us recommit ourselves to being stewards of the Earth and champions for its creatures, both big and small.

Thank you

International Women's Day 08 March

Ladies and gentlemen, students, and esteemed staff,

Today, as we gather to commemorate International Women's Day, we celebrate the remarkable achievements and contributions of women throughout history. It is a day to honour their resilience, courage, and determination in shaping our world.

International Women's Day has a rich history dating back over a century, originating from the labour movement in the early 20th century. It serves as a reminder of the ongoing struggle for gender equality and women's rights. As the suffragettes fought for the right to vote and countless women campaigned for equal rights and opportunities, their legacy continues to inspire us today.

The importance of this day cannot be overstated. It is a time to reflect on the progress we have made and the work that still lies ahead. It is a call to action to break down barriers, challenge stereotypes, and empower women and girls worldwide. As Malala Yousafzai once said, "We cannot all succeed when half of us is held back."

There are countless ways to celebrate International Women's Day, both big and small. From organizing events and marches to highlighting the achievements of women in various fields, every action makes a difference. It is also a day to amplify the voices of women, listen to their stories, and stand in solidarity with them.

But beyond the celebrations, there are valuable lessons to be learned from International Women's Day. It teaches us the importance of inclusivity, diversity, and equality. It reminds us that gender should never be a barrier to opportunity and that everyone deserves a seat at the table. As Ruth Bader Ginsburg famously said, "Women belong in all places where decisions are being made."

As we commemorate International Women's Day, let us commit ourselves to creating a more equitable and just society. Let us continue to champion the rights of women and girls, advocate for gender equality in all aspects of life, and strive to build a world where every individual can thrive regardless of gender.

In the words of Maya Angelou, "Each time a woman stands up for herself, without knowing it possibly, without claiming it, she stands up for all women." Let us stand together, today and every day, in support of women's rights and gender equality.

*** Thank you ***

World Water Day
22 March

Ladies and gentlemen, esteemed students and staff,

As we gather here today, on this auspicious occasion of World Water Day, it is with great reverence that we acknowledge the paramount significance of this essential element in sustaining life on our planet. As the renowned environmentalist, Jacques Yves Cousteau, once remarked, "Water and air, the two essential fluids on which all life depends, have become global garbage cans." These words poignantly encapsulate the profound importance of water in our lives and the urgent need to protect it.

Throughout history, water has been revered and cherished by civilizations around the world. From the ancient civilizations that thrived along the banks of great rivers to the modern cities built around vast oceans, water has been the lifeblood of human existence. Its role in agriculture, industry, and daily sustenance cannot be overstated. However, despite its critical importance, water resources are increasingly under threat due to pollution, overuse, and climate change.

Today, as we commemorate World Water Day, we are called upon to reflect on our collective responsibility towards water conservation and stewardship. It is not merely a matter of environmental concern but also a moral imperative to ensure that every individual has access to clean and safe water. As the Dalai Lama aptly stated, "Access to clean water is a fundamental human right." Therefore, it is incumbent upon us to take concrete actions to protect and preserve this precious resource for present and future generations.

Celebrating World Water Day is not merely a symbolic gesture but an opportunity to instil a culture of conservation and sustainability within our community. There are numerous ways in which we can actively participate in this endeavour. From reducing our water consumption through simple lifestyle changes to advocating for policies that promote responsible water management, each of us has a role to play in safeguarding our water resources.

Moreover, World Water Day serves as a reminder of the interconnectedness of all life forms on Earth. Just as water flows freely across borders and boundaries, so too must our efforts to address water-related challenges be collaborative and inclusive. As the African proverb wisely states, "If you want to go fast, go alone. If you want to go far, go together." By fostering partnerships and cooperation at local, national, and global levels, we can collectively work towards ensuring water security for all.

In conclusion, let us heed the words of Margaret Atwood, who eloquently said, "Water is to me, I confess, a phenomenon which continually awakens new feelings of wonder as often as I view it." Let us approach World Water Day with a sense of wonder, gratitude, and commitment to protecting this invaluable resource. Together, let us strive to create a world where every drop of water is cherished, respected, and preserved for generations to come.

Thank you

International Day of Zero Waste 30 March

Ladies and gentlemen, esteemed faculty members, and dear students,

I stand before you today with a heart brimming with enthusiasm as we gather to celebrate a cause that holds immense significance not only for our school but for the entire planet. Today marks the International Day of Zero Waste, a day dedicated to raising awareness about the importance of reducing, reusing, and recycling to minimize our impact on the environment.

The history of this day traces back to the growing global concern over the staggering amount of waste produced by human activities and its devastating effects on ecosystems worldwide. Recognizing the urgency of the situation, the international community came together to advocate for sustainable solutions to combat the growing waste crisis.

Zero Waste Day serves as a poignant reminder of our collective responsibility to safeguard the environment for future generations. It prompts us to reflect on our consumption habits and encourages us to adopt more eco-friendly practices in our daily lives.

The importance of this day cannot be overstated. By striving towards zero waste, we not only mitigate the environmental damage caused by excessive consumption and disposal but also contribute to the conservation of natural resources and the preservation of biodiversity. Each small step we take towards reducing our waste footprint makes a meaningful difference in the fight against climate change and pollution.

Now, you may be wondering, how can we celebrate Zero Waste Day in a meaningful way? Well, there are countless ways we can participate and make a positive impact. We can organize waste reduction workshops, promote composting and recycling initiatives, or even embark on a campus-wide clean-up campaign. The key is to foster a culture of environmental stewardship and empower each other to take action.

As educators, we have a profound responsibility to instil in our students the values of sustainability and environmental consciousness. By integrating environmental education into our curriculum and providing opportunities for hands-on learning, we can equip our students with the knowledge and skills they need to become responsible stewards of the planet.

Furthermore, Zero Waste Day serves as a valuable opportunity for us to reflect on the lessons we can learn from nature itself. Nature operates in a circular economy, where waste is transformed into valuable resources through processes like decomposition and regeneration. As we strive towards zero waste, let us draw inspiration from nature's ingenuity and strive to emulate its efficiency in our own lives.

In conclusion, Zero Waste Day is a powerful reminder of our shared responsibility to protect and preserve the planet. As we commemorate this day, let us reaffirm our commitment to reducing waste, conserving resources, and building a more sustainable future for generations to come.

Thank you for your attention, and let us all pledge to make every day a Zero Waste Day.

World Health Day
07 April

Ladies and gentlemen, esteemed faculty, and dear students,

Today, on the occasion of World Health Day, we come together to reflect on the significance of this day, its history, ways to celebrate, and the lessons it imparts. As we gather here, let us remember the words of Mahatma Gandhi, who said, "It is health that is real wealth and not pieces of gold and silver." These words resonate deeply, especially in the challenging times we are living in.

World Health Day, celebrated annually on April 7th, marks the founding of the World Health Organization (WHO) in 1948. It serves as an opportunity to draw global attention to important health issues and encourage action to promote healthier living. This year's theme, like many before it, underscores the urgency of addressing pressing health concerns and striving for equitable access to healthcare for all.

As we commemorate this day, let us not forget the various ways we can celebrate and contribute to the promotion of health and well-being. Simple acts, such as adopting healthy lifestyle habits, promoting hygiene practices, and supporting community health initiatives, can make a significant difference. Remember, as Florence Nightingale once said, "Health is not only to be well, but to be able to use well every power we have."

In our school community, we have a responsibility to instil habits that foster good health among our students and staff. Let us continue to prioritize physical activity, nutritious eating, and mental wellness in our curriculum and daily routines. By creating a supportive environment that promotes healthy behaviours, we empower our students to make positive choices that will benefit them throughout their lives.

Furthermore, let us use this day as an opportunity to reflect on the lessons learned from recent global health crises. The COVID-19 pandemic has taught us invaluable lessons about the importance of preparedness, resilience, and solidarity in the face of health challenges. As we navigate the ongoing pandemic and its aftermath, let us remain vigilant and proactive in safeguarding the health and well-being of our school community.

In conclusion, let us recommit ourselves to the pursuit of health and wellness for all. As Nelson Mandela once said, "Health cannot be a question of income; it is a fundamental human right." Let us work together to ensure that every member of our school community has the opportunity to thrive and live a healthy, fulfilling life.

Thank you for your attention, and let us continue to strive for a healthier, happier future for all.

International Mother Earth Day 22 April

Ladies and gentlemen, esteemed students, and dedicated staff,

Today, as we gather to celebrate International Mother Earth Day, it's imperative to reflect on the significance of this occasion and our collective responsibility towards our planet. As Margaret Mead once said, "Earth provides enough to satisfy every man's needs, but not every man's greed." These words resonate deeply, urging us to reevaluate our relationship with the environment and to strive for a sustainable future.

International Mother Earth Day traces its roots back to the early 1970s when environmental movements gained momentum worldwide. On April 22nd, 1970, millions took to the streets to protest environmental degradation and advocate for change. Inspired by this global outcry, the United Nations designated April 22nd as a day to raise awareness about environmental issues and promote environmental action.

Today, we honour this tradition by engaging in various activities that promote environmental awareness and conservation. From tree-planting initiatives to recycling drives, every action, no matter how small, contributes to the greater good. As Mahatma Gandhi famously said, "The earth, the air, the land, and the water are not an inheritance from our forefathers but on loan from our children. So, we have to handover to them at least as it was handed over to us."

Furthermore, International Mother Earth Day serves as a poignant reminder of the interconnectedness of all living beings. Just as the health of our planet affects every aspect of our lives, our actions, too, have far-reaching consequences. As John Muir eloquently put it, "When one tugs at a single thing in nature, he finds it attached to the rest of the world."

Today, let us commit ourselves to being stewards of the earth, to protect and preserve its natural beauty for generations to come. Let us embrace sustainable practices in our daily lives, from reducing waste to conserving energy. As Wangari Maathai once said, "In a few decades, the relationship between the environment, resources, and conflict may seem almost as obvious as the connection we see today between human rights, democracy, and peace."

In conclusion, as we commemorate International Mother Earth Day, let us remember that the earth is not just our home; it is a precious gift entrusted to our care. Let us heed the wisdom of indigenous cultures who teach us to live in harmony with nature, for in doing so, we ensure a brighter future for all. As Chief Seattle famously said, "The earth does not belong to us; we belong to the earth." Let us honour this truth today and every day.

Thank you

International Day of Families 15 May

Ladies and gentlemen, esteemed faculty, dear students, and honoured guests,

As we gather here today on this auspicious occasion of the International Day of Families, celebrated globally on May 15th, it is my privilege to address you on the significance of this day, its history, and ways we can celebrate and reflect on the lessons it imparts.

The International Day of Families was proclaimed by the United Nations General Assembly in 1993 to highlight the importance of families as the basic unit of society. Families serve as the foundation of our communities, providing love, support, and guidance to each member. They are the cornerstones of our society, shaping individuals and influencing future generations.

Throughout history, families have played a vital role in nurturing values, traditions, and cultural heritage. They provide a sense of belonging, stability, and security, fostering emotional well-being and resilience in times of adversity. It is within the family unit that we learn essential life skills, develop our identity, and form lasting bonds that transcend time and distance.

On this day, we celebrate the diversity of families around the world, recognizing that families come in various forms, shapes, and sizes. Whether it's nuclear families, extended families, single-parent families, or chosen families, each one is unique and deserves to be honoured and respected.

There are numerous ways we can celebrate the International Day of Families within our school community. We can organize family-themed activities and events, such as family picnics, storytelling sessions, or workshops on parenting and family dynamics. These activities not only bring families closer together but also foster a sense of unity and belonging within our school community.

Furthermore, this day serves as a reminder to cherish and appreciate our own families. It's an opportunity to spend quality time with loved ones, express gratitude for their love and support, and strengthen the bonds that bind us together. Simple gestures, such as sharing a meal, engaging in meaningful conversations, or participating in recreational activities, can help reinforce the importance of family in our lives.

As we celebrate the International Day of Families, let us also reflect on the valuable lessons that families teach us. They teach us the importance of love, compassion, and empathy. They instil values of respect, tolerance, and cooperation, which are essential for building harmonious relationships and inclusive communities. Moreover, families teach us resilience, perseverance, and the power of unity in overcoming challenges and adversities.

In conclusion, the International Day of Families serves as a poignant reminder of the vital role that families play in our lives and society. It is a day to celebrate, honour, and cherish our families, as well as reflect on the lessons they impart. Let us embrace the diversity of families around the world and strive to create nurturing, supportive environments where every family feels valued and respected.

Thank you for your attention, and may we all continue to uphold the importance of families in shaping a brighter future for generations to come.

World No. Tobacco Day
31 May

Dear Students and Esteemed Staff,

I stand before you today on the occasion of World No Tobacco Day, observed annually on the 31st of May, to shed light on the significance of this day, its history, ways to commemorate it, and the invaluable lessons it imparts.

World No Tobacco Day serves as a global platform to raise awareness about the harmful effects of tobacco use and second-hand smoke exposure. It underscores the urgent need for effective policies to reduce tobacco consumption and promote public health. Tobacco use remains one of the leading causes of preventable death worldwide, claiming millions of lives each year. By observing this day, we reaffirm our commitment to building a tobacco-free world for current and future generations.

World No Tobacco Day was established by the World Health Organization (WHO) in 1987 to draw attention to the tobacco epidemic and its devastating health consequences. Since then, it has evolved into a crucial annual event, uniting governments, public health organizations, and communities worldwide in the fight against tobacco. The day also marks the anniversary of the WHO's adoption of the Framework Convention on Tobacco Control in 2003, a landmark treaty aimed at reducing tobacco-related illnesses and deaths.

There are numerous ways to commemorate World No Tobacco Day and contribute to its objectives:

Educational Campaigns: Organize informative sessions and workshops to educate students and staff about the dangers of tobacco use, addiction, and the benefits of quitting.

Community Outreach: Engage in outreach activities to spread awareness beyond the school walls, such as hosting awareness drives, distributing educational materials, or organizing anti-tobacco rallies.

Support for Smokers: Offer support and resources for those who wish to quit smoking, such as cessation programs, counselling services, and access to nicotine replacement therapies.

Policy Advocacy: Advocate for strong tobacco control policies at the local, national, and international levels, including smoke-free environments, tobacco advertising bans, and increased taxation on tobacco products.

Promotion of Healthy Alternatives: Encourage the adoption of healthy lifestyle choices and alternatives to tobacco use, such as regular physical activity, nutritious diet, and stress management techniques.

On this World No Tobacco Day, let us reflect on the following lessons:

Health is Wealth: Our health is our most precious asset, and tobacco use poses a significant threat to it. By prioritizing our well-being and making informed choices, we can lead healthier, more fulfilling lives.

Individual Responsibility: Each of us has a role to play in combating the tobacco epidemic, whether by choosing not to smoke, supporting loved ones in their quit attempts, or advocating for tobacco control policies in our communities.

Collective Action: Realizing a tobacco-free world requires collective action and collaboration across sectors. By working together, we can create environments that promote health and well-being for all.

In conclusion, let us seize the opportunity presented by World No Tobacco Day to reaffirm our commitment to a smoke-free future. Together, let us empower ourselves and others to make healthier choices, protect our communities from the harms of tobacco, and strive towards a world where every individual can thrive free from the burden of tobacco-related diseases.

Thank you

Global Day of Parents
01 June

Dear students and staff,

Good morning! Today, we gather to celebrate a very special occasion, the Global Day of Parents, observed annually on the 1st of June. This day serves as a poignant reminder of the invaluable role parents play in the lives of children and the importance of nurturing strong family bonds.

The history of the Global Day of Parents dates back to 2012 when the United Nations General Assembly proclaimed it as a day to honour parents worldwide. It recognizes their selfless commitment to raising children and acknowledges the crucial role they play in providing love, guidance, and support to their families.

As we celebrate this day, it's essential to reflect on the significance of parental involvement in education. Research consistently shows that when parents are actively engaged in their children's schooling, students are more likely to perform better academically, have higher self-esteem, and exhibit positive behaviour both in and out of the classroom.

So, how can we celebrate this day? There are countless ways to show appreciation for our parents. Whether it's a simple thank-you note, a heartfelt conversation, or a small gesture of kindness, every expression of gratitude matters. Let's take this opportunity to express our love and appreciation for the unwavering support our parents provide each day.

Furthermore, let's use this day as a reminder to strengthen our relationships with our families. Spend quality time together, engage in meaningful conversations, and create lasting memories. Remember, our parents are our first teachers, and there is much wisdom to be gained from their experiences and guidance.

On this Global Day of Parents, let's also reflect on the valuable lessons they have taught us. From the importance of honesty and integrity to the power of resilience and perseverance, our parents have instilled in us the values that shape our character and guide our actions.

As members of our school community, let's also extend our appreciation to the parents of our students. Their partnership and collaboration are essential in creating a supportive and nurturing learning environment where every child can thrive.

In conclusion, let us cherish and celebrate the remarkable bond between parents and children. Today and every day, let's express our gratitude for the love, sacrifice, and dedication of our parents. Together, let's continue to build strong families, vibrant communities, and a brighter future for all.

Thank you

World Environment Day
05 June

Ladies and gentlemen, esteemed students and staff,

As we gather here today on the auspicious occasion of World Environment Day, celebrated globally on June 5th, it's a moment of reflection and action. This day holds a significant place in our hearts and minds as it reminds us of our responsibility towards our planet, our home.

To truly appreciate the importance of this day, let us delve into its history. World Environment Day was established by the United Nations General Assembly in 1972, marking the beginning of a global movement to raise awareness and take positive action for the protection of our environment. Over the years, it has grown into a powerful platform for advocacy, engagement, and collective action.

The theme for this year's World Environment Day is "Eco-Restoration," emphasizing the urgent need to restore ecosystems that have been degraded or destroyed. As stewards of this planet, it is incumbent upon us to take concrete steps towards rejuvenating our environment and preserving it for future generations.

In the words of Margaret Mead, "Never doubt that a small group of thoughtful, committed citizens can change the world; indeed, it's the only thing that ever has." Each one of us has the power to make a difference, no matter how small our actions may seem. Whether it's reducing our carbon footprint, conserving water, or advocating for sustainable practices, every effort counts.

Today, I urge each and every one of you to reflect on the impact of our actions on the environment and to pledge to make positive changes in our daily lives. Let us plant trees, clean up our surroundings, and embrace eco-friendly practices in all aspects of our lives.

As Mahatma Gandhi famously said, "The earth, the air, the land, and the water are not an inheritance from our forefathers but on loan from our children. So, we have to handover to them at least as it was handed over to us." Let us be mindful of our responsibility to preserve and protect our planet for future generations.

In conclusion, let us celebrate World Environment Day not just today, but every day, by living in harmony with nature and embracing sustainable practices. Together, let us be the change we wish to see in the world.

Thank you

World Day Against Child Labour 12 June

Ladies and gentlemen, students and staff,

Today, we gather here on a significant occasion - the World Day Against Child Labour. It's a day when we reflect on the importance of eradicating child labour, a practice that deprives children of their childhood, their potential, and their dignity. As we commemorate this day, let us delve into its history, understand its importance, explore ways to celebrate, and draw lessons that can guide us in our efforts to combat this global issue.

The history of the World Day Against Child Labour dates back to 2002 when the International Labour Organization (ILO) initiated this observance to raise awareness and mobilize efforts to eliminate child labour. Since then, it has served as a platform for governments, organizations, and individuals worldwide to advocate for the rights of children and to promote policies and actions that protect them from exploitation.

The importance of this day cannot be overstated. Child labour not only robs children of their right to education, play, and a nurturing environment but also perpetuates cycles of poverty and inequality. It denies them the opportunity to develop physically, mentally, and emotionally, hindering their potential to become productive members of society. By addressing child labour, we not only uphold the fundamental rights of children but also contribute to building a more just and equitable world for all.

Now, let's discuss ways to celebrate this day and contribute to its objectives. First and foremost, education is key. We must educate ourselves and others about the realities of child labour, its causes, and its consequences. This can be done through workshops, seminars, and educational campaigns aimed at raising awareness and fostering dialogue within our community.

Secondly, advocacy plays a crucial role. We can use our voices to advocate for policies and practices that protect children from exploitation and promote their rights to education, health, and well-being. By engaging with policymakers, stakeholders, and the public, we can influence change at local, national, and international levels.

Thirdly, action is imperative. Whether through volunteering, supporting organizations working on the ground, or implementing child-friendly practices in our own lives and workplaces, each of us can make a difference. By taking concrete steps to prevent and address child labour, we contribute to building a safer, more inclusive world for children everywhere.

Lastly, let us draw lessons from this observance that can guide us in our ongoing efforts to combat child labour. We must recognize that eradicating child labour requires a multi-faceted approach that addresses its root causes, including poverty, lack of access to education, and social inequality. It demands collaboration, coordination, and commitment from all sectors of society - government, civil society, businesses, and individuals alike. Most importantly, it requires empathy and compassion for the millions of children around the world who continue to toil in hazardous conditions, often invisible and voiceless.

In conclusion, as we mark the World Day Against Child Labour, let us reaffirm our commitment to protecting the rights and dignity of every child. Let us strive to create a world where every child can enjoy their childhood, pursue their dreams, and reach their full potential. Together, let us work towards a future free from child labour, where every child is given the opportunity to thrive.

Thank you

International Day of Yoga
21 June

Dear Students and Staff,

Good morning! Today, we gather here to celebrate the International Day of Yoga, observed globally on June 21st. Yoga, an ancient practice that originated in India, holds profound significance for our physical, mental, and spiritual well-being. As we commemorate this day, let us delve into the history, importance, ways to celebrate, and the lessons we can learn from yoga.

Yoga traces its roots back over 5,000 years ago to the Indus-Sarasvati civilization in Northern India. It was first mentioned in the Rig Veda, the oldest sacred texts of Hinduism. Over time, yoga evolved into various forms and practices, each aimed at harmonizing the body, mind, and spirit. In the 20th century, yoga gained popularity worldwide, thanks to pioneers like Swami Vivekananda and later, influential teachers such as B.K.S. Iyengar and K. Pattabhi Jois.

The significance of yoga extends far beyond physical exercise. It is a holistic practice that promotes inner peace, mindfulness, and balance. Through yoga, we cultivate self-awareness, discipline, and resilience. It teaches us to embrace challenges with equanimity and find harmony amidst the chaos of modern life. Furthermore, yoga fosters a sense of unity and interconnectedness with all living beings, emphasizing compassion and empathy.

There are numerous ways to celebrate the International Day of Yoga. We can start the day with a collective yoga session, led by experienced instructors or our own skilled practitioners within the school community. Additionally, we can organize workshops, seminars, and discussions to deepen our understanding of yoga philosophy and its practical applications in daily life. Encouraging students to participate in creative activities such as poster-making contests or essay competitions centred around yoga can also foster engagement and enthusiasm.

Yoga imparts invaluable lessons that resonate both on and off the mat. It teaches us the importance of breath awareness, mindfulness, and being present in the moment. Through yoga postures (asanas), we learn to challenge ourselves while honouring our bodies' limitations. The practice of meditation cultivates mental clarity, emotional stability, and resilience in the face of adversity. Moreover, yoga instils virtues such as patience, perseverance, and gratitude, nurturing our holistic growth as individuals.

In conclusion, as we celebrate the International Day of Yoga, let us remember that yoga is not just an exercise routine but a profound journey of self-discovery and transformation. Let us embrace its teachings with open hearts and minds, incorporating them into our daily lives to lead happier, healthier, and more fulfilling existence. Together, let us embark on this journey of wellness, unity, and enlightenment.

Thank you, and Namaste!

International Youth Day
12 August

Ladies and gentlemen, students, and esteemed staff,

As we gather here today on the auspicious occasion of International Youth Day, it is with great pride and excitement that I address you all. International Youth Day, celebrated annually on the 12th of August, serves as a global platform to recognize the power, potential, and contribution of young people to society. It is a day to celebrate the energy, creativity, and resilience of our youth, as well as to reflect on the challenges they face and the opportunities they deserve.

The history of International Youth Day dates back to the year 2000 when the United Nations General Assembly designated this day as a means to raise awareness of the challenges and issues facing the world's youth. Since then, it has become an occasion for governments, organizations, and communities around the world to come together and celebrate the positive impact that young people have on our world.

The importance of International Youth Day cannot be overstated. Our youth represent the future leaders, innovators, and change-makers of tomorrow. They possess a unique perspective, boundless energy, and a desire to make a difference in the world. It is essential that we support and empower them to realize their full potential and become active participants in shaping the future.

There are numerous ways to celebrate International Youth Day and honour the contributions of our young people. We can organize events and activities that highlight their achievements, talents, and initiatives. We can create opportunities for dialogue and engagement, where young people can voice their concerns, ideas, and aspirations. We can also provide them with access to resources, mentorship, and support systems to help them succeed in their endeavours.

As we celebrate International Youth Day, there are several valuable lessons that we can learn from our youth. Their optimism, idealism, and courage remind us of the importance of dreaming big and pursuing our passions fearlessly. Their resilience, adaptability, and willingness to embrace change inspire us to overcome challenges and seize opportunities for growth and development. And their commitment to social justice, equality, and sustainability serves as a powerful reminder of our collective responsibility to create a better world for future generations.

In conclusion, International Youth Day is a time for us to celebrate the incredible potential and contributions of our youth, as well as to reflect on the lessons they teach us. Let us pledge to support and empower our young people, to listen to their voices, and to work together towards a brighter and more inclusive future for all.

Thank you

World Humanitarian Day
19 August

Ladies and gentlemen, esteemed students, and dedicated staff,

As we gather here today, on the occasion of World Humanitarian Day, it is my honour to address you on the significance of this day and the profound impact it holds for humanity. August 19th is not just another date on the calendar; it is a day that reminds us of our collective responsibility towards each other, regardless of nationality, race, or creed.

History teaches us that World Humanitarian Day commemorates the tragic loss of lives, including those of humanitarian workers, in the 2003 bombing of the United Nations headquarters in Baghdad. It serves as a stark reminder of the sacrifices made by individuals who dedicate their lives to helping others in need, often in dangerous and challenging environments.

Today, we honour their memory by reaffirming our commitment to compassion, empathy, and service to others. It is a day to recognize the importance of humanitarian action and to acknowledge the tireless efforts of those who work tirelessly to alleviate suffering and promote peace and justice around the world.

As members of this school community, we have a unique opportunity to make a difference, both locally and globally. Whether through acts of kindness, volunteering, or raising awareness about pressing humanitarian issues, each one of us has the power to create positive change.

There are numerous ways to celebrate World Humanitarian Day. We can organize fundraisers to support humanitarian organizations, engage in community service projects, or participate in educational activities to learn more about global challenges and solutions. By coming together as a school community, we can amplify our impact and contribute to a more compassionate and just world.

In the words of Mahatma Gandhi, "The best way to find yourself is to lose yourself in the service of others." Let us heed these words and strive to embody the spirit of compassion and solidarity in all that we do.

As we commemorate World Humanitarian Day, let us also reflect on the lessons it teaches us. It reminds us of the importance of empathy, cooperation, and standing up for what is right. It challenges us to think beyond ourselves and to consider the needs of others, especially those who are most vulnerable and marginalized.

In conclusion, let us seize this opportunity to honour the legacy of humanitarian heroes, both past and present, by committing ourselves to acts of kindness, service, and advocacy. Together, we can build a brighter future for all.

Thank you for your attention, and let us continue to strive towards a more compassionate and inclusive world.

90

International Day of Peace
21 September

Ladies and gentlemen, esteemed students and staff,

Today, as we gather to commemorate the International Day of Peace, it is an honour for me to address you all. This day, observed on the 21st of September each year, holds immense significance as it calls for global ceasefire and non-violence. It serves as a reminder of the power of peace, unity, and understanding in our world.

Reflecting on the history of this day, we are reminded of its origins in 1981 when the United Nations General Assembly declared the International Day of Peace to coincide with its opening session. Since then, this day has been dedicated to promoting the ideals of peace, both within and among all nations and peoples.

In celebrating this day, there are countless ways in which we can contribute to the cause of peace. From fostering empathy and compassion in our daily interactions to engaging in acts of kindness and reconciliation, each one of us has the ability to make a positive difference. Whether it's through organizing peace-themed events, participating in community service projects, or simply spreading messages of harmony and understanding, our collective efforts can pave the way for a more peaceful world.

Moreover, the International Day of Peace provides us with valuable lessons that we can carry forward in our lives. It teaches us the importance of dialogue over conflict, cooperation over division, and tolerance over prejudice. It reminds us that peace is not merely the absence of war, but the presence of justice, equality, and respect for human rights. It encourages us to embrace diversity, celebrate our differences, and strive for unity amidst our various backgrounds and beliefs.

As we mark this day, let us also take a moment to reflect on the challenges that continue to threaten peace in our world. From armed conflicts and humanitarian crises to social injustices and environmental degradation, the need for peace and solidarity has never been greater. It is up to each one of us to stand up against violence and injustice, to advocate for peace and reconciliation, and to work towards building a more peaceful and sustainable future for generations to come.

In conclusion, let us pledge to uphold the ideals of peace not just today, but every day of the year. Let us commit ourselves to being agents of positive change in our communities and beyond. And let us never forget that in our pursuit of peace, we are not alone - we stand together, united in our shared vision of a world where every individual can live in dignity, freedom, and harmony.

Thank you

91

International Day of Older Persons 01 October

Ladies and gentlemen, esteemed students and staff,

Today, as we gather to commemorate the International Day of Older Persons, we celebrate the wisdom, experience, and invaluable contributions of our elders to our community and society at large. This day holds profound significance as it reminds us to honour and respect the elders among us, who have paved the way for our present and future.

History teaches us that throughout civilizations, older persons have been revered for their wisdom and guidance. In many cultures, elders hold positions of leadership and authority, offering invaluable insights garnered through years of experience. Their stories, traditions, and knowledge form the cornerstone of our collective heritage, passing down wisdom from one generation to the next.

As we celebrate this day, let us reflect on the ways we can honour and show gratitude to our older community members. Simple gestures such as spending time with them, listening to their stories, or seeking their advice can go a long way in making them feel valued and appreciated. It is essential to recognize that aging is a natural part of life, and with it comes a wealth of experience and wisdom that enriches us all.

There are various ways we can celebrate the International Day of Older Persons within our school community. We can organize intergenerational activities where students and older adults come together to share their experiences, hobbies, and talents. These interactions foster meaningful connections and break down generational barriers, promoting understanding and empathy.

Furthermore, we can engage in community service projects aimed at supporting older persons in need. Whether it's volunteering at a nursing home, organizing a fundraiser for elderly care facilities, or simply reaching out to isolated seniors, these acts of kindness demonstrate our commitment to ensuring the well-being of our older community members.

As we commemorate this day, let us also reflect on the lessons we can learn from our elders. Their resilience in the face of adversity, their commitment to family and community, and their unwavering optimism serve as inspiration to us all. By embracing their values and incorporating them into our lives, we can cultivate a culture of respect, compassion, and inclusion.

In conclusion, the International Day of Older Persons serves as a reminder to honour and celebrate the invaluable contributions of our elders. Let us seize this opportunity to express our gratitude, engage in meaningful interactions, and learn from their experiences. Together, let us create a world where older persons are cherished, respected, and empowered to live fulfilling lives.

Thank you

92

International Day of Non-Violence 02 October

Ladies and gentlemen, esteemed students, faculty members, and staff,

Today, as we gather here on this significant occasion of the International Day of Non-Violence, commemorating the birthday of Mahatma Gandhi, we are reminded of the enduring power of peace and the profound impact of non-violent resistance in shaping our world.

Mahatma Gandhi, often hailed as the Father of our Nation, embodied the principles of non-violence and peaceful resistance like no other. His unwavering commitment to truth and justice, his tireless efforts in advocating for the oppressed, and his profound belief in the inherent dignity of every individual continue to inspire generations across the globe.

On this day, we not only honour the legacy of Gandhi Ji but also reaffirm our collective commitment to fostering a culture of peace, tolerance, and understanding within our school community and beyond.

History bears witness to the transformative power of non-violence in effecting social change. From the civil rights movement led by Martin Luther King Jr. to the struggle against apartheid in South Africa, non-violent resistance has been instrumental in bringing about positive and lasting transformations in society.

As we commemorate this day, let us reflect on the ways in which we can incorporate the principles of non-violence into our daily lives. It is about more than just the absence of physical violence; it is about cultivating empathy, compassion, and respect for one another. It is about finding constructive ways to resolve conflicts and address injustices without resorting to aggression or hostility.

There are various ways in which we can celebrate this day and contribute to the promotion of non-violence. We can organize discussions and workshops to raise awareness about the importance of peaceful conflict resolution. We can engage in acts of kindness and solidarity within our community, reaching out to those in need and offering support and comfort. We can also educate ourselves about the struggles faced by marginalized communities around the world and stand in solidarity with them in their quest for justice and equality.

Moreover, let us not forget the invaluable lessons that non-violence teaches us - the power of resilience in the face of adversity, the strength of unity in diversity, and the belief in the inherent goodness of humanity. These are lessons that will serve us well not only in our academic pursuits but also in our personal and professional lives.

As we mark this International Day of Non-Violence, let us recommit ourselves to the noble ideals espoused by Mahatma Gandhi and strive to be beacons of peace and harmony in our society. Let us be the change that we wish to see in the world, and together, let us build a brighter and more compassionate future for all.

*** Thank you ***

World Habitat Day
07 October

Dear Students and Esteemed Staff Members,

I stand before you today with a sense of urgency and purpose as we gather to commemorate World Habitat Day, celebrated annually on October 7th. This day holds immense significance in our global calendar, as it serves as a reminder of the critical role habitats play in our lives and the importance of sustainable development for the well-being of current and future generations.

World Habitat Day was first established by the United Nations General Assembly in 1985 to reflect on the state of our towns and cities and the basic right of all to adequate shelter. It serves as a platform to raise awareness about the need for sustainable urbanization and the provision of adequate housing for all. Today, as we face unprecedented challenges such as climate change, rapid urbanization, and environmental degradation, the message of World Habitat Day resonates more strongly than ever.

There are numerous ways in which we can celebrate World Habitat Day and contribute to its objectives. As individuals, we can start by reflecting on our own habits and consumption patterns, ensuring that we minimize waste and reduce our carbon footprint. Additionally, we can participate in community clean-up initiatives, tree planting drives, and advocacy campaigns to promote sustainable living practices.

As a school community, we can integrate lessons on environmental stewardship and sustainable development into our curriculum, fostering a culture of responsibility and respect for our planet. We can also organize educational events, guest lectures, and workshops to raise awareness about the importance of habitat preservation and the interconnectedness of human and environmental health.

On this World Habitat Day, let us reflect on the lessons learned from our past actions and commit to building a more sustainable future. We have seen firsthand the consequences of unchecked urbanization and unsustainable development - from habitat loss and biodiversity decline to natural disasters and climate-induced displacement. It is imperative that we take decisive action to address these challenges and ensure that our cities and communities are resilient, inclusive, and environmentally sustainable.

In conclusion, let us use this World Habitat Day as an opportunity to renew our commitment to the principles of sustainable development and equitable access to housing and basic services for all. Together, let us work towards creating a world where every individual has a safe and dignified place to call home, and where our habitats are thriving, resilient, and in harmony with nature.

Thank you for your attention, and let us continue to strive towards a better tomorrow for ourselves and future generations.

94

United Nations Day
24 October

Ladies and gentlemen, esteemed students and staff,

Today, as we gather to commemorate United Nations Day, we are reminded of the profound significance of unity, cooperation, and peace on a global scale. On this day, we celebrate the establishment of the United Nations, an organization founded on the principles of diplomacy, human rights, and international cooperation.

The history of the United Nations is one of resilience, hope, and determination. In the aftermath of World War II, nations came together with a shared vision: to prevent future conflicts, promote social progress, and foster a better world for all. Since its inception, the UN has played a pivotal role in addressing global challenges, from poverty and hunger to climate change and conflict resolution.

As we mark this day, it is crucial to reflect on the ways in which we can contribute to the ideals and objectives of the United Nations. Each of us has a role to play in promoting peace, justice, and equality in our communities and beyond. Whether through volunteerism, advocacy, or simply embracing diversity, we can all make a difference in building a more inclusive and sustainable world.

There are numerous ways in which we can celebrate United Nations Day within our school community. We can organize educational workshops and discussions to raise awareness about the UN's work and its impact on our lives. We can also engage in cultural exchanges, showcasing the rich diversity of our global community and celebrating the traditions and customs of different nations.

Furthermore, we can use this day as an opportunity to reaffirm our commitment to the principles of the United Nations. Let us pledge to uphold human rights, promote tolerance and understanding, and work towards the common good. By embracing these values, we can contribute to a more peaceful and prosperous world for generations to come.

In commemorating United Nations Day, we are reminded of the lessons we can learn from the past and the challenges that lie ahead. Let us draw inspiration from the courage and conviction of those who have come before us, and let us stand united in our efforts to build a better future for all.

As we celebrate United Nations Day, let us recommit ourselves to the ideals of peace, cooperation, and solidarity. Together, we can make a difference and create a world where every voice is heard, and every person is valued.

Thank you, and let us continue to strive for a brighter tomorrow.

World Science Day for Peace and Development 10 Nov.

Ladies and gentlemen, esteemed students, and dedicated staff members,

As we gather here today, on the auspicious occasion of World Science Day for Peace and Development, celebrated annually on November 10th, it is my privilege to address you on the significance of this day, its historical context, ways to celebrate, and the invaluable lessons it offers us all.

In the words of the renowned physicist and Nobel laureate, Albert Einstein, "Peace cannot be kept by force; it can only be achieved by understanding." This sentiment lies at the heart of World Science Day for Peace and Development. Established by UNESCO in 2001, this day serves as a reminder of the pivotal role that science plays in fostering peace and sustainable development worldwide.

Throughout history, scientific advancements have often been at the forefront of progress, paving the way for innovation, cooperation, and ultimately, peace. From the discovery of penicillin by Alexander Fleming to the invention of the Internet by Tim Berners-Lee, science has continuously transcended borders, bringing people together in pursuit of shared goals and aspirations.

Today, as we commemorate World Science Day, let us reflect on the ways in which science has contributed to the betterment of humanity and explore ways to harness its power for the greater good. From tackling climate change and global health crises to promoting gender equality and social justice, there is no shortage of challenges that science can help us address.

To celebrate this day, I encourage each and every one of you to engage in activities that promote scientific inquiry, critical thinking, and collaboration. Whether it's conducting experiments in the laboratory, organizing educational workshops, or participating in community outreach initiatives, let us seize this opportunity to ignite a passion for science and inspire positive change in our world.

Moreover, let us not forget the invaluable lessons that World Science Day imparts upon us. As we strive for peace and development, let us remember that progress is not a solitary endeavour but rather a collective journey. By embracing diversity, fostering inclusivity, and upholding the principles of equity and justice, we can create a more harmonious and sustainable future for generations to come.

In closing, let me leave you with a quote from another distinguished scientist, Marie Curie, who once said, "Nothing in life is to be feared; it is only to be understood." On this World Science Day for Peace and Development, may we continue to seek understanding, promote cooperation, and work together towards a brighter tomorrow.

Thank you

96

World Children's Day
20 November

Good morning esteemed students and staff,

Today, as we gather on this special occasion of World Children's Day, we celebrate the essence of childhood, the beacon of hope, and the promise of our future. It is a day dedicated to you, the young minds shaping our world, and to reaffirm our commitment to nurturing and safeguarding your rights, aspirations, and dreams.

World Children's Day holds profound significance as it marks the anniversary of the United Nations General Assembly's adoption of the Declaration of the Rights of the Child in 1959 and the Convention on the Rights of the Child in 1989. These seminal documents underscore the fundamental rights of every child - the right to education, protection, healthcare, and a nurturing environment. As Nelson Mandela aptly stated, "There can be no keener revelation of a society's soul than the way in which it treats its children."

Reflecting on history, we recognize the strides made in championing children's rights globally. From the establishment of educational reforms to the enactment of child labour laws, our collective efforts have transformed the landscape for children worldwide. However, challenges persist, reminding us of the imperative to remain vigilant and steadfast in our advocacy for children's rights.

On this auspicious day, let us recommit ourselves to the welfare of children in our community and beyond. Here are a few ways we can celebrate World Children's Day:

Education Empowerment: Let us pledge to provide equitable access to quality education, ensuring that every child has the opportunity to learn, grow, and thrive.

Child Advocacy: Let us raise our voices against injustices such as child labour, trafficking, and exploitation, and advocate for policies that safeguard the well-being of children.

Empathy and Compassion: Let us foster a culture of empathy and compassion, nurturing environments where children feel valued, respected, and loved.

Creative Expression: Let us encourage children to express themselves creatively through art, music, and storytelling, empowering them to share their unique perspectives with the world.

Community Engagement: Let us engage with our local communities to address the needs of vulnerable children, fostering partnerships and collaborations that create positive change.

As we celebrate World Children's Day, let us reflect on the lesson's children teach us - lessons of resilience, curiosity, and boundless imagination. In the words of Kofi Annan, "There is no trust more sacred than the one the world holds with children. There is no duty more important than ensuring that their rights are respected, that their welfare is protected, that their lives are free from fear and want and that they can grow up in peace."

In conclusion, let us stand in solidarity with children worldwide, affirming our commitment to building a future where every child can realize their full potential. As we celebrate World Children's Day, may we remember that the true measure of our society's greatness lies in how we nurture and uplift the youngest among us.

Thank you

World AIDS Day
01 December

Ladies and gentlemen, students and staff,

Today, as we gather here on this significant day, World AIDS Day, we come together to remember, to educate, and to unite in our efforts to combat HIV/AIDS. It is a day of reflection, awareness, and action. As the principal of this esteemed institution, I stand before you not just as an educator, but as an advocate for health, compassion, and understanding.

Thirty-eight years ago, on December 1, 1988, World AIDS Day was first observed, initiated by the World Health Organization, to raise awareness about the HIV/AIDS pandemic and to mourn those we have lost. Since then, this day has served as a reminder of the devastating impact of this disease on individuals, families, and communities worldwide.

As we commemorate this day, it's essential to reflect on the progress we've made and the challenges that remain. The theme for this year's World AIDS Day, "Ending the HIV/AIDS Epidemic: Equitable Access, Everyone's Voice," underscores the importance of ensuring access to HIV prevention, treatment, care, and support for all, without discrimination.

In the words of Nelson Mandela, a champion in the fight against HIV/AIDS, "AIDS is no longer just a disease; it is a human rights issue." Indeed, stigma and discrimination continue to be significant barriers in our efforts to end the HIV/AIDS epidemic. It is our collective responsibility to challenge misconceptions, foster empathy, and create a supportive environment for those affected by HIV/AIDS.

Prevention remains our most potent tool in the fight against HIV/AIDS. Education is key. We must empower ourselves with knowledge about safer sex practices, the importance of regular testing, and the use of pre-exposure prophylaxis (PrEP) and post-exposure prophylaxis (PEP). As educators, it's our duty to equip our students with the information and skills they need to protect themselves and others.

But prevention goes beyond just individual behaviour. It also involves addressing social determinants such as poverty, inequality, and gender-based violence that fuel the spread of HIV/AIDS. As Martin Luther King Jr. once said, "Injustice anywhere is a threat to justice everywhere." We must advocate for policies and programs that promote social justice and address the underlying factors driving the HIV/AIDS epidemic.

Moreover, we must never forget the lessons of the past. The early days of the HIV/AIDS crisis were marked by fear, silence, and inaction. Countless lives were lost due to ignorance and neglect. We cannot afford to repeat the mistakes of the past. We must remain vigilant, proactive, and compassionate in our response to HIV/AIDS.

In closing, let us remember that the fight against HIV/AIDS is not over. It requires our continued commitment, solidarity, and determination. As Desmond Tutu once said, "Do your little bit of good where you are; it's those little bits of good put together that overwhelm the world." Together, let us stand united in our efforts to end the HIV/AIDS epidemic once and for all.

Thank you

98

International Day for the Abolition of Slavery 02 Dec.

Ladies and gentlemen, esteemed faculty members, and dear students,

Today, we gather here to commemorate the International Day for the Abolition of Slavery, observed annually on December 2nd. As we reflect on this solemn occasion, it's imperative to recognize the significance of acknowledging our past, understanding its impact on our present, and collectively striving towards a future free from the shackles of exploitation and oppression.

In the words of Nelson Mandela, "To deny people their human rights are to challenge their very humanity." The history of slavery is a dark chapter in humanity's story-a chapter marked by cruelty, exploitation, and the denial of basic human dignity. From the transatlantic slave trade to modern-day forms of servitude, slavery has taken various forms, but its fundamental injustice remains unchanged.

As educators and students, it is our responsibility to confront this painful history head-on and to ensure that the lessons learned are not forgotten. We must educate ourselves and others about the horrors of slavery, fostering empathy and understanding, and cultivating a deep commitment to human rights and social justice.

Preventing the resurgence of slavery requires vigilance, activism, and international cooperation. We must advocate for policies that protect the rights of the most vulnerable in our society and hold accountable those who seek to exploit others for profit. As Mahatma Gandhi famously said, "The best way to find yourself is to lose yourself in the service of others." Let us heed his words and dedicate ourselves to the fight against modern-day slavery in all its forms.

Moreover, as members of a global community, we must recognize that slavery knows no borders. It is a scourge that affects every corner of the world, transcending race, religion, and nationality. Therefore, it is incumbent upon us to work together across cultures and continents to eradicate this grave injustice once and for all.

In closing, let us remember that the struggle for freedom and equality is ongoing. On this International Day for the Abolition of Slavery, let us recommit ourselves to the pursuit of a world where every individual can live with dignity, liberty, and justice. As Frederick Douglass eloquently stated, "Without a struggle, there can be no progress." May we continue to strive for progress and justice for all.

Thank you

99

Human Rights Day
10 December

Ladies and gentlemen, esteemed students, faculty, and staff,

Today, on December 10th, we come together to commemorate International Human Rights Day, a day that holds profound significance in the collective consciousness of humanity. It is a day to reflect on the universal rights and freedoms that every individual is entitled to, regardless of race, religion, gender, or any other characteristic.

As Nelson Mandela once said, "To deny people their human rights are to challenge their very humanity." This sentiment encapsulates the essence of why we observe this day. Human rights are not just abstract principles; they are the foundation of a just and equitable society, where every person can live with dignity and respect.

History reminds us of the atrocities committed when human rights are disregarded. From the horrors of slavery to the genocide of the Holocaust, history serves as a poignant reminder of the consequences of allowing hatred and discrimination to flourish unchecked. Yet, it also serves as a testament to the resilience of the human spirit and the power of individuals and communities to bring about change.

Observing International Human Rights Day is not merely a symbolic gesture; it is a call to action. It is a reminder that we each have a role to play in upholding and defending human rights, both in our own communities and on the global stage. Whether it's speaking out against injustice, advocating for marginalized groups, or simply treating others with kindness and compassion, every action we take matters.

There are many ways we can observe this day and contribute to the promotion of human rights. We can educate ourselves and others about the Universal Declaration of Human Rights, adopted by the United Nations General Assembly in 1948. Its timeless principles continue to serve as a guiding light for the protection of human dignity around the world.

We can also engage in acts of solidarity with those whose rights are being violated. Whether it's attending rallies, signing petitions, or supporting organizations working to advance human rights causes, our collective voice has the power to effect change.

Furthermore, we must recognize that the struggle for human rights is ongoing and that progress is not inevitable. It requires constant vigilance and commitment from each and every one of us. As Eleanor Roosevelt, one of the driving forces behind the Universal Declaration of Human Rights, famously said, "Where, after all, do universal human rights begin? In small places, close to home."

In closing, let us reaffirm our commitment to upholding the inherent dignity and worth of every individual. Let us stand together in solidarity with all those who continue to fight for their rights, and let us never forget that the quest for justice and equality is a journey that we must embark on together.

Thank you

World Basketball Day
21 December

Ladies and gentlemen, esteemed students, and dedicated staff members,

As we gather today on this auspicious occasion of World Basketball Day, observed globally on December 21st, I am reminded of the profound impact this sport has had on individuals and communities around the world. Just as the game itself is a fusion of skill, teamwork, and passion, it symbolizes values that extend far beyond the court.

As the renowned basketball coach Phil Jackson once said, "The strength of the team is each individual member. The strength of each member is the team." This sentiment encapsulates the essence of basketball - a sport that not only celebrates individual talent but thrives on collaboration and unity. Whether you're dribbling the ball down the court or cheering from the sidelines, every member of the team plays a crucial role in achieving success.

But beyond the realm of athletics, basketball serves as a powerful vehicle for social change and empowerment. Throughout history, it has been a catalyst for breaking down barriers and fostering inclusivity. From the pioneering efforts of players like Kareem Abdul-Jabbar and Bill Russell to the global phenomenon of the NBA, basketball has transcended cultural, racial, and geographical boundaries, inspiring generations of fans and athletes alike.

Moreover, basketball teaches us valuable life lessons that extend far beyond the final buzzer. It teaches us resilience in the face of adversity, discipline in the pursuit of excellence, and perseverance in the pursuit of our goals. As Michael Jordan famously remarked, "I've failed over and over and over again in my life. And that is why I succeed." These words remind us that setbacks are merely opportunities for growth, and success is born out of determination and resilience.

Today, as we celebrate World Basketball Day, let us not only honour the rich history and tradition of this beloved sport but also reaffirm our commitment to embodying its timeless values of teamwork, perseverance, and inclusivity. Whether we're shooting hoops on the court or tackling challenges in our daily lives, let us remember that together, we are capable of achieving greatness.

In closing, I leave you with the words of legendary basketball coach John Wooden, who said, "It's not so important who starts the game but who finishes it." As we embark on this journey together, let us strive to finish strong, both on and off the court.

Thank you, and let's make today a slam dunk of celebration for World Basketball Day!

www.ingramcontent.com/pod-product-compliance
Lightning Source LLC
LaVergne TN
LVHW061540070526
838199LV00077B/6852